PIVOT & GROW

THE ESSENTIAL BUSINESS SUCCESS GUIDE

W&M

PIVOT & GROW 1

First published in November 2020

Writing Matters Publishing

ISBN 978-1-912774-73-9

Editor: Andrew Priestley

A CIP catalogue record for this book is available from the British Library.

All people mentioned in case studies have been used with permission, and/or have had names, genders, industries and personal details altered to protect client confidentiality.

Please join the *Leadership Gigs* group on LinkedIn.

Contents

There Has Never Been A Time Like This

Foreword: Paul Dunn Co-Founder B1G1

Since April 1981, I've been privileged to be able to speak passionately on stages around the world. And I'm fortunate enough to win awards. But more importantly, I'm especially fortunate that audiences seem to love what I do too.

And all these years, I have had a problem. It's this: I can never (as in seriously never) do the same presentation twice.

But I have frequently used the same opening slide. It says this in large text:

There has never been a time like this.

And of course, it's always been true. It's true no matter what day it is; every moment has its one specialness.

But today as I write this some 6 months in to a global pandemic, that 8-word phrase has never been truer.

And that's because the pandemic has brought with it an acceleration of moments and a collection — perhaps even a collision — of moments that you and I have never experienced in our lifetimes — and mine goes back to 1943!

It's ravaged economies. There have been nearly 30 million people with the virus and almost a million have died. It's impacted millions. It's ripped loved ones from families and friends.

And yes, businesses have closed. Bankruptcies have soared.

Yet, as is always the case with tragedy, there's another side.

And it's that side that we visit in *Pivot and Grow.*

It's a side where business owners have finally stopped the busy-ness of business and done what legend Michael Gerber first exhorted them to do in 1990 with his 'WORK ON, NOT IN' mantra.

I still remember getting Michael's *E-Myth* book in December 1990 and thinking, "Oh my God. I just have to get on the fax (yes, it was that long ago) and invite him to Australia to speak to our clients."

And it's taken this long for that mantra to really sink in with record numbers of people — many *forced* to work from home and ponder questions like:

- Can we ever get back on track OR should we be on a new track? Am I on the right track?
- Does this business still make sense ... in this form?
- If my customers problems have changed, does that mean I should develop new solutions?

And of course the answer to that last question is a definite *Yes!!!!* It's fundamental. Any business, yours and mine, exists to add enormous value to customers by giving them great solutions to challenges they face. So if the challenges change, solutions you sell must also change or be *re-packaged* in some way.

Enter one of the key words of 2020 (together with *unprecedented* and *you're on mute*) PIVOT.

It's not often you read it and GROW together. This book changes that.

You'll see how business owners and their teams have done precisely that. They've changed tack (and track) AND they've grown... many times by huge amounts.

How they've done it will inspire you.

And, who knows, they might even move you to pivot and grow too.

And what a pure joy that would be for so many — your customers, your team, your family, your community and indeed, our world.

Entrepreneurs really *do* change our world.

And now, more than ever, humanity needs you to lead that change. And guess what? There's never been a time like this to do it.

Paul Dunn

Co-Founder Buy One Give One (B1G1)
www.b1g1.com

The Magic Within

Nikie Piper

Awareness is the first step to creating change. I think you will agree with me here, but what you're also probably thinking is, 'Yes, I know that, but how does that help me?'

From my own journey, I notice that so often we forget the basics and the simple solutions, so intent are we on diving into any issues and problems and the *doing* of things in our business. We strive to prove that we are the best or that we don't need any help or we're just too busy to take the time to invest in ourselves. We all have that list of *nice to haves* or *one days* or *things to do when everything else is right first.*

One fundamental of life is that you cannot support others if you don't support yourself first. You are the key and you are the answer.

Before you skip this as an *alternative* view or *woo woo stuff* in search of more concrete solutions, let me ask you a couple of questions. *What if your thoughts really did create your reality? What if your thoughts really did become things?* Would it not be worth your time to learn more about how you can create a positive change to your life and your business? As Tony

Robbins so eloquently says, 'Energy flows where attention goes.' How many people are aware of their energy outside of their personal feelings, and especially in the world of business. It can be difficult to pay attention to your personal energy level and its effect on your business prosperity while your thoughts are wrapped up in the day and life of the business and always moving on to the next thing.

Maybe most will never think about the energy in and around their business or even how that affects their business. There is perhaps, this never-ending focus of attention on the bottom line, and fixing issues and problems become the focus. Don't get me wrong, I know just how important it is to find solutions to these.

What I am saying is that if you focus on what's going right, what you're grateful for within your life and your business and shift your attention from lack and negative you change the whole energy around the situation. Quite literally as Tony Robbins says, 'Energy flows where attention goes.'

As the whole world finds itself recovering from the pandemic, you're perhaps feeling frustrated, lost, possibly devastated, overwhelmed, even lonely and wondering how on earth you are going to survive. Perhaps unconsciously looking for that magic pill, fix, button, course, cash injection or person (or anything!) to make everything OK?

The last thing on your mind is being grateful for anything or looking at your energy and least of all the energy of your business. You just want answers, right?

But wait a minute, doesn't like attract like? Yes?

Like attracts like.

So, what is it that you do want to attract? Are you the person that can attract it? Are your personal core beliefs and values aligned with that of your business? And with your ideal clients? What are your business core beliefs and values? Do they sit well with you?

Creating a positive yet supportive, collaborative environment will create such a shift in how you see your people and your business. That in turn will reflect not only on you, your staff and the business, it will also increase positive energy and draw more of the right sort of clients. People buy from people they know, like and trust that they feel can solve their problems.

Who are your people, your ideal clients, your perfect business partners, and your perfect team? What are you grateful for about them? Are you aligned with them? Think about how you perceive them.

Some businesses fail to define their *people*. This potentially means they are unclear how exactly they help their customers. Therefore, any activity for that business is like shooting in the dark; sometimes they win, but most of the time they lose.

Every customer counts, every customer wants to feel like you value their contribution to your business, they want to feel special. Every customer wants to be aligned to what you are offering. Every customer wants to be thanked, however small their purchase.

Include in this, every person in your business and your business: treat your business as a person. Treat your customers, your staff and the business as you would treat your best friend. Pay attention to the energy, the thoughts that get created and flow through. Awareness is the first step to change.

Pivot your thinking: grow your business. You may well ask how, and quite simply you can only come from a place of your own truth. Your business is a reflection of you and those in it.

Get really clear. Do you need to get back to basics?

Take time to review what is it exactly that you offer. What are your products? Check that you haven't diverged so far from your core offering that you don't know what it is anymore. Reassess how each product supports your perfect clients.

As you conduct your review, ask yourself these questions: *Are you grateful for your products? Grateful for the problem or issues that those products solve for your clients? How can you serve your clients more? Have you asked them? Are you grateful to serve them? Do you recognise that every client has a choice?*

Gratitude. A simple, but vastly effective solution. Gratitude is a pivotal skill for everyone, especially in business, and regardless of age it is a simple step that can have a profound impact. Even during times of crisis and change there are always lessons to learn and things to be grateful for.

A Radical Thought...

Gratitude isn't just one more thing to do, it's a lifestyle choice and a game changer. Gratitude is also a business strategy and a tool for growth.

Gratitude can go a long, long way to improve the quality of

your life and your business. Why not try it, you have nothing to lose? Be conscious of removing any focus that pulls you towards the angst and the lack, the lack of money, the lack of customers or the bills piling up. Focus instead on what is needed to create an energy that is more conducive to moving forward, this provides so many more benefits than it first appears.

By changing the focus, the focus changes.

Focus in on what is going well, what has been sold, how great the team is, how grateful you are to any suppliers, customers, stock, money coming in, the restructures and redefinition of your business. Be grateful for it all and remember that it's not to belittle those negative or perhaps scary or overwhelming feelings or not to take them into consideration. Not at all, but rather refocus where your thoughts and energy are.

From the 'old master' Lao-Tzu 'Change your thoughts change your life' What can you focus on that you're totally grateful for? Once you move into gratitude things start to show up differently. In reality you see the same things, but it's your reaction to them that's different. In other words, it's not what you've got but how you think about what you've got.

- Can you move into being grateful for your business?
- What has it given you in the past?
- What does it give you now?
- What has it allowed you to do?
- What are you grateful for that you wouldn't have without your business?

- What are the lessons you've learned from your business, the people that you've met, the products you've created, the money that has come into your business?
- Think about the premises, your location, your logos, your designs, your products, your people.

What can you be grateful for? There is always, always something to be grateful for. Think about it, write it down. You can change your energy around your situation. Being grateful changes your mood and your emotions, which in turn changes your energy and your thought processes and in turn what you attract. Like attracts like.

You've got nothing to lose by giving it a go! Energy flows where your attention goes. You can change your energy, change your mindset, change your thoughts around your current situation, move it away from lack, and remove the words *not* and *can't* from your vocabulary. There's abundance everywhere, even in the driest of situations. If you are willing to look you will see with different eyes and thoughts.

The magic within you is your secret weapon, your ability to focus on what is going well, being grateful for what you have and shifting the energy.

Believe in better, trust in better, expect better and know that better is coming. Energy is everything; everything is made from energy. Be grateful for what you have, and you shall receive more.

You always have a choice and it does help to remember that. At the end of the day, everything comes down to the quality and reflection of your own personal energy, thoughts and beliefs.

You never know just how far reaching your words or actions can be, how much impact they will have on someone and how much they could change someone's life.

If I can empower even just one person to change the way they think about their life, their business, their situation or their future and to see their world differently then I am truly grateful to have been of service.

About Nikie Piper

Nikie has first-hand experience at creating her life with her thoughts and using the power of gratitude and intention to do so. Rising from the depths of depression, twice being made redundant from a job she loved and separating from her husband of 24 years. It took all her positive thinking, mental fitness and positive action to climb out of over £60,000 worth of outstanding debt and relying on friends to support her.

Throughout this time Nikie started to journal and born out of frustration with not being able to find anything on the market that fulfilled her journaling needs, Nikie created her own range of gratitude and daily journals, using her stunning gift in photography. Nikie is the owner and founder of My Awesome Life Ltd, through which she now guides, teaches, and empowers others in changing their *traditional* thinking habits through proven processes, online programs, live events and books.

Contact Nikie Piper

Website: *www.nikiepiper.com*

Facebook: *www.facebook.com/nikie.piper*

LinkedIn: *www.linkedin.com/in/nikie-piper-coach*

awesome@nikiepiper.com

Pivot With Profit

Andy Cristin

Currently there is a lot of talk about businesses pivoting as we come out of lockdown. The term refers to a strategy change using a metaphor from the world of sport. In basketball a pivot is where a player changes direction keeping one foot planted on the ground and swivelling the other to face a different direction.

In business we tend to think of pivot being a change of strategy where some parts of the business are maintained, but other parts are changed. Working as a finance director I've been involved with a number of businesses who have pivoted both successfully and unsuccessfully. These pivots were generally either a change in service (or product), or a change in the client type, but never both at the same time.

Three common types of pivot are:

1. Existing Services, New Clients

In this strategy a business finds a new market for an existing product or service. Examples of this include Play-Doh which was originally designed as a cleaning product for removing coal residue from wallpaper, but found a whole new market as a modelling clay for art & crafts and Airbnb which was originally designed for the conference market before the business switched tack and saw more opportunity serving the retail travel market.

Play-Doh and Airbnb's revenues increased significantly after finding a new client base, but in my experience this type of pivot has been more of a defensive strategy helping businesses to survive after a drop in demand. For example, a client in the construction sector foresaw a reduction in revenues when the trend for building out-of-town retail centres in the UK reduced following the 2008 financial crisis. By marketing their services to other parts of the construction industry they were able to weather the storm and survive, but they did so with reduced revenues and margins. It bought them time though and eventually they re-built their business.

2. Existing Clients, New Services

This strategy is more radical, marketing a completely new service to the existing client base. There have been a number of famous pivots of this type, such as the chewing gum manufacturer Wrigley. The business started out selling baking powder and giving away free chewing gum to promote sales. Over time the company saw more interest in the free gum than in the baking powder that they were promoting. Wrigley switched focus to market and sell gum and it became the largest gum manufacturer in the world.

In my experience however, this type of pivot has never been successful. It's one thing to convince new clients that your services can work for them, but quite a different challenge to deliver something completely new to your existing clientele.

3. Existing Clients, Improved Services

The third strategy also focusses on existing clients, but in this case rather than try to offer something completely new the original service is developed to provide a better solution. Often this involves narrowing down the service to hone in on a niche solution.

An example of this strategy is Netflix. More than two decades ago the business started out as a movie rental service. Customers ordered films on Netflix's website and received DVDs in the post a few days later. Once they had watched the films they returned them in envelopes provided. In those days it was like a mail order version of Blockbusters. Later on the streaming of films was made available in multiple countries and more recently the company has been producing its own content as a producer and distributor of films and television series. By comparison, Blockbusters didn't do so well.

The most successful businesses that I have worked with have followed similar strategies. Often it took more than one change in direction, but by really understanding their market's requirements and making adjustments to the service offerings, significant growth in revenue and profits were achieved.

Other types of pivot can also be successful, such as changes in sales or distribution channels. In my consultancy business I have used a mixture of more focussed services and a change in distribution channel (Zoom meetings rather than in person meetings) since lockdown and this has been an improvement for me and my clients.

Once you've decided on the type of pivot you are going to make, the five tips below will help you execute it successfully. They are based on my experience as a finance director advising small and medium sized businesses.

1. Define And Communicate The Changes You Are Making

Write down a brief but concise summary of the changes you are going to make. This could be in the form of an executive summary for a business plan (about two pages) outlining the changes and how they affect different parts of the business. This is more important in businesses where there are multiple decision-makers, but even if you work alone it will help you stay focussed.

If appropriate communicate these changes to potential clients. For example a small firm of architects who had seen revenue from the retail sector diminishing might decide to replace that business by specialising in changing office space, unwanted after lockdown, into residential units. Putting case studies and videos on their website, alongside their other services, would be a good way to signal to the market that they are able to provide these services while still remaining open to general architectural projects.

2. Know Your Numbers

Make sure you understand where the profit will come from after making your pivot. In most cases your cost structure will have changed and you need to understand your new costs in detail. Make sure you know what the variable costs of each transaction or project are expected to be and separately compute the fixed overheads that the business will incur regardless of the volume of transactions.

Your pricing may also have changed and it is important to clarify the new gross profit and net profit expectations. Produce a mini profit and loss account for one transaction, or one project, so that you can see clearly how the new business is going to perform. It may well be worth discussing the numbers with your accountant before going any further. If there's not enough profit in this idea, stop now and think again.

3. Plan Ahead

Once you are happy that you can make a profit on a transactional basis, produce a plan for the next 12 months to show how the volumes of transactions increase over time. While each individual transaction might make gross profit, in the first few months you may not have sufficient sales to cover all of your fixed overheads. It is important to understand what the breakeven point is and what level of sales are required to make a profit. You will also need to include any extra costs such as new sales and marketing expenditure, but also think about historic costs which you may now be able to reduce.

Most of my clients have moved to home-working as a consequence of the pandemic. Some lost revenue and others had to cope with increased costs just to continue in business. All these changes affected the profitability of these businesses and need to be factored into their planning. How will your business's profitability change?

4. Keep A Close Eye On The Cash

With a plan for the next 12 months and a good understanding of your breakeven point, the next task is to produce a robust cash flow forecast. If you are making a significant pivot, or if you need to make a large investment it is quite likely that you will have negative cash flow initially.

It's a well-known fact that even profitable businesses can fail due to a lack of cash. The problem is even more likely when making a big change in the business. Make sure that your assumptions are not too optimistic and allow for a contingency in your cash flow projections.

Monitor your cash flows against your projections every week at the beginning. If you can see that you are not achieving your targets at least you will have bought yourself time to make changes and put things right.

5. Look For Marginal Gains

Finally, look for opportunities to improve your profitability and cash flow. If your business has previously given clients 30 days' credit, could you move to payment in advance by direct debit for your new service? The benefits are both an improvement in cash flow and a reduction in expenses to chase overdue debtors. Alternatively, (or even additionally) could you obtain extended credit terms from suppliers?

Have a good look at the costs that your business is incurring before you make your changes and identify any costs that you will not need in the future. Could you outsource some tasks at a lower cost than in-house?

Is there an opportunity to improve your revenue? If your pricing was historically based on hourly rates could you increase your rates? Better still could you improve your profitability using value pricing?

Conclusion

There's not much point in making changes to your business unless they improve your profitability. To be successful get confidence in your numbers, plan ahead and monitor your progress regularly.

References:

- Hiskey, D. (n.d.). The shocking story behind Playdoh's original purpose. [online] Business Insider.
- Aydin, R. (2019). The history of Airbnb, from air mattresses to $31 billion company - Business Insider.
- chcom (2013). Wrigley's. [online] Companies History - The biggest companies in the world.
- Hosch, W.L. (2019). Netflix, Inc. | American company. In: Encyclopædia Britannica. [online]

About Andy Cristin

Andy Cristin is a finance director with over 25 years' experience of working with a broad range of commercial organisations in the UK, Europe and the Middle East.

He has worked in two FTSE-listed companies, and has also been involved with eleven start-ups, four of which grew from nothing to become multi-million pound businesses.

In 2008, Andy founded Pareto Financial Direction Ltd, which focusses on business owners in the B2B services sector, helping them to understand their numbers and build better businesses.

Andy is the author of *The Profit Mindset* and is a contributor to various business related publications.

Contact Andy Cristin

Website: www.pareto-fd.com

LinkedIn: www.linkedin.com/in/andycristin

Cutting Through When Seemingly Cut Down:

Lessons From Lockdown About (Re)Building Your Brand, Your Business And Yourself

Kerry Collinge

I love Caitlin Moran. At the time of writing she is on a press tour ahead of the release of her next book *More Than a Woman* (Moran C. Ebury Press 2020). Her whole career has been about capturing moments where people, particularly women, often through hilarious experiences, pivot and grow. She writes: "Back when I finished writing *How to Be a Woman* a decade ago, I truly thought I had it all figured out. I thought I had vanquished the patriarchy in my mind and nailed the general 'hoo-ha' of becoming a woman. I firmly believed 'the difficult bit' was over, and my forties were going to be a doddle. If only I'd known when middle age arrives, a whole new bunch of tough questions need answering". This is so very, very true. Amidst the ongoing uncertainties that 2020 has brought to all of us, none of us feel this more than now on both a universal and personal level. Just when I thought I had come through a particularly challenging five years, finally feeling settled geographically and landing a perfect role with an amazing team at a fantastic new Health and Beauty company, I thought that my 'difficult bit' was over. But then Coronavirus was gifted to the world and stuck two fingers up at both the Beauty Industry and at me. My role was made redundant.

I would have expected nothing less. The CEO's instinct for building business was the very basis on which I chose the role. At my interview I asked, "How would you describe your business philosophy?".

The CEO responded with this story:

"When the recession of 2008/9 hit, we were a fledgling company, with an amazing product in a sea of Beauty Giants with deep pockets. However, many of our competitors panicked. They were afraid. But I saw this as an opportunity for growth. I invested in a new, stealth sales team and equipped them with cutting edge equipment to help our customers retain their business in those difficult times. And it paid off. That gamble earnt us loyalty, which resulted in long-term business growth".

He then went on to say that he needed me in his organisation because he had "grown despite his marketing". What I heard in his story was the very opposite. This was a business and a leader who had great vision and instinctively knew what all great business leaders should know; a recession is a huge marketing opportunity. I immediately asked where I could sign up.

That CEO was acting on instinct rather than classical marketing training, and so he would not have described it this way, but his strategy was about being distinctive through innovation and using market fluctuations to gain *extra share of voice* (ESOV). By offering his customers a point of difference at a time they could be struggling, he grew both their businesses and his, gaining long term loyalty and thereby sales. This is the very basis of great marketing. Businesses and brands that find ways to gain ESOV are proven to be the ones to grow long term. When lockdown hit and 95% of his customers were forced to close shop entirely, our CEO re-enacted the same strategy – new innovation and new ways to serve customers – this time in a digital world. But he also knew he had to cut all costs he could in order to protect his business and the newly created role of marketing director had to go.

'Keeping the Light On' is the most important strategy in difficult times. Rather than retrenching investment, true leaders see the opportunity. To invest in innovative ways to better be present and serve your customers at a time when many will pull back investment, meaning that your share of voice will be greater, as the cost of going to market is cheaper. For larger brands who advertise, because demand for media space goes down, you get more space for your money. And the same is true for smaller brands who are vying for space in customer's hearts and minds. Bryon Sharpe's oft cited How Brands Grow (Oxford University Press - 2010), would call this Mental Availability. To grow your business and brand you must find ways to get more space in your customers hearts and minds. Recession offers this and great marketeers remember the lessons from history:

- Advertising investment has long-term impacts on business growth

- Untrained competitors will cut marketing spend
- Your share of voice will increase relative to your competitors as a result
- If you don't cut ad spend (or even increase ad spend) you will achieve long-term growth

Therefore, your role as a business or marketing leader, is to keep reminding yourself that marketing is an investment rather than a cost.Those that invest in recession, will be the ones that win and grow in the long term.

And the same is true of your personal brand. In times of recession or redundancy, it would be easy to go dark and give in to feelings of failure and fear, but it's critical you keep the light on. Find new and innovative ways to use your talents to reach a potential new employer or even speak to new clients which might help you set up your own business. Learn new skills. Even write about your experience as a springboard to something new.

In her 2019 book *Wolfpack* (Piatkus and Celadon Books), Amy Wambach, Olympic Gold Medallist and holder of the record for the most international soccer goals ever scored (male or female), talks to her readers about how her failures helped lead her to her calling. She strongly believes that "Fear is Fuel". She tells the story of how when she retired from international football, she was afraid, as she did not leave her career with the same financial nest egg as her male counterparts. She realised she had to start career all over again, working out what her transferable talents were. Humiliatingly, she failed in front of the whole world at her new chosen career as a commentator for ESPN during the

2016 UEFA European Championship. On live TV, in front of millions of people, she realised she freezes in front of a camera. But from the ashes of that shame, she founded her leadership business and now talks vulnerably and openly to the world about her new rules for female leadership. One of which is *Failure means you are IN the game*.

Through lockdown, we have seen so many examples of brands and businesses that have used perceived failure to pivot and grow: the gap year student I met on a walk who couldn't travel and so used her savings to set up a pop-up 'Lockdown Café' near Henley and now has over 12 times her savings; The CEO of award-winning coffee company TrueStart, and former client, who lost her retail business but set her mind to both taking her business online to keep some cash flow to feed her family, whilst also bravely speaking out about how her perceived struggles with mental health were actually a blessing when it came to seeing things differently and building a business; and the friend who has a new child-focussed bathroom brand called Scrubbington's, who told me one night over a warm wine on the banks of the Thames about her obsession with finding a kinder way than alcohol to sanitise our children's hands (Scrubbington's 'Bug Off' sanitiser launched in July 2020 – alcohol and bug free!). All of these brands and businesses used the fear of failure during the Coronavirus crisis to press the reset button, and have gained extra saliency and share of voice, thus setting themselves up to win in the long term.

Something that has returned to mind during the pandemic is *The Hero's Journey* by Joseph Campbell. *The Hero with a Thousand Faces,* written in 1949 (NewWorld Library) explains the universal motif of adventure and transformation that runs through all of the world's mythic traditions. Campbell's 12-step journey inspired George Lucas's Star Wars stories and rings as true for brands and businesses as it does for life itself.

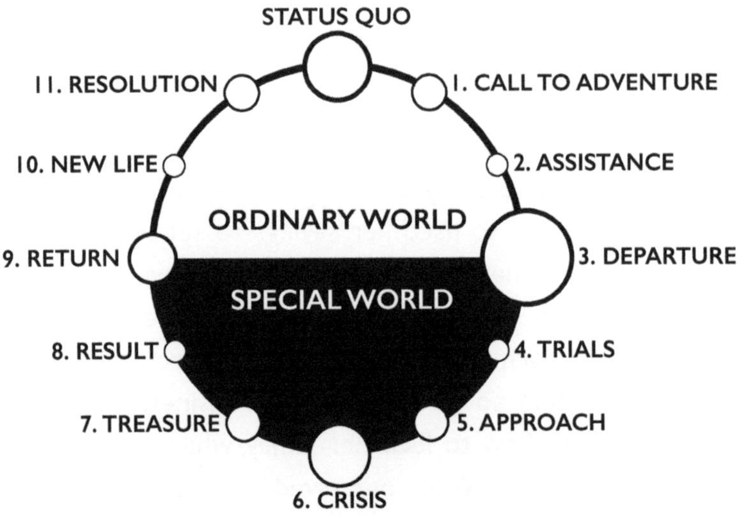

There has to be an event (pandemic) that jolts you out of the ordinary, and a challenge to rise to, in order to cross the threshold to reward and resurrection. There are those that will refuse the call and remain in what they think is the ordinary world, only to realise that world has gone forever. Those who stopped, retrenched, retracted investment, waiting for a *return to normal*, will likely only find a world moved on. Those who look for ideas, mentors and face into the test, pivoting their approach, will likely find personal and business growth.

When we think back on 2020, we should not remember the pain of lockdown, but the opportunities it offered us; a chance to reconnect with friends and families, or to connect differently with them, to improve our health and fitness, to remember the pleasure of taking time to cook for the family rather than eat out and an opportunity to listen hard to our souls and rewrite our personal landscapes both at home and in business.

Then there must be the gratitude many of us will feel towards the brave leaders of businesses staring at the costs and returns of a sudden halt in revenues, against the monthly wage bill multiplied by an unknown number of weeks and months of lockdown, against money in the bank. When faced with this adversity and the potential collapse of their hard-earnt businesses (and also the jobs of their employees and their families who depended on it) many brave leaders were up all many nights, quickly resetting their thinking in order to save their businesses and the livelihoods of their employees. Working out how they could increase their salience and share of voice to serve their customers to ensure long-term growth.

On a personal level, resetting from the perceived shame and hopelessness of redundancy has been about a *growth* mindset. Picking yourself up, learning from what happened and realising that failure is fuel for growth has been key. The day I was let go from my role, I revisited my vision and realised that ego had let me take on a role that wasn't my path. The critical learning has been that nothing is forever, but the learning you can get even in short periods of times is a gift. *The difficult bit* is never over. It is about the journey and not the destination.

In the past few months I taken the opportunity to pause and invest in myself. And I have seen nothing but opportunity all around me; new paths opening up, new ideas, new people coming into my life to help and guide, careers I had never considered before, new courage to be vulnerable and to reach out and chat to networks, old and new, asking if they can help and taking the chance to write for the first time since university. Seeing entrepreneurs grabbing this *new normal* to create new brands, I have decided to pivot and refocus my talents on serving emerging ethical brands and business leaders to become more than just commercial products, helping them work out how to cut through, increase their voice and grow.

About Kerry Collinge

Kerry Collinge is a branding and communications expert with over 20 years' experience working with both blue-chip multinationals and start-ups on marketing strategy and planning. She has worked as a Marketing and Communications Director for brands from beer to luxury beauty. Her calling card is often her work on both Cadbury Gorilla and London 2012 Olympics, but her passion is using her training, talents and skills from big corporates to support entrepreneurs to create and grow brands that are looking to make a difference in the world – for people or the planet. Recent work has included helping establish an award-winning, sustainable, "wild for life" coffee brand, founding a kid focussed food brand infused with extra vitamins and minerals and delivering Immunity Intelligence Pods to market in the first three weeks of the Coronavirus Pandemic. She is a founding partner at Marketing Consultancy Earth to Cosmos.

Contact Kerry Collinge

Kerry@theglow.london

www.theglow.london

+44 (0) 7792 178889

A Parent Company: Three Keys To Managing Your Children So You Can Manage Your Business Better

Amber Trueblood, MBA, LMFT

It's tough enough to grow a successful business amidst the current economic uncertainty without trying to do it while your children learn social studies on a Zoom call in the next room. *That's like attempting to clean your kitchen counter with a piece of raw chicken.* Even for the most focused and organized entrepreneurs, the idea of parenting without *normal* school, sports, clubs and playdates is utterly daunting.

The good news is, you already possess most of the skills and tools you need.

The bad news is, if you don't take a purposeful approach to this new world of parenting, then your business, family and sanity may suffer.

As a therapist and mom of four sons, I've experienced my share of frustration and overwhelm. I vividly remember sitting at home with a newborn, a two-year-old, a three-year-old and a five-year-old. I felt exhausted but bored.

I was surrounded by humans but felt isolated. I was brain-fogged but craved a mental challenge. And, I was chubby on the outside but starved on the inside.

After feeding myself a decade's worth of books, seminars, retreats, workshops and meditations, I launched a company, homeschooled my four boys and wrote my first book. The shift happened quickly but as they say, *an overnight success takes years*. I merely uncovered simple, effective practices that allowed me to enjoy myself while creating a life that works best for me.

If you incorporate the simple tools described below, you can better manage your personal life in order to better manage your business life:

The First Key: Maximize Your Mindset

How you mentally approach your day, your family and your business affects how you perceive the world and how you respond as a result of those perceptions. Your mental mindset can shift everything. Good or Bad.

Ever sleep terribly, wake with a weird pain in your shoulder, realize you're out of coffee, about to be late for a meeting, and then step on a rogue Lego piece? Chances are, you won't be in the best state of mind for that meeting.

Try these three tricks to Maximize Your Mindset:

1. **Breathe Deeply.** Take 10 minutes at the start of your day to breathe slowly and deeply, without devices or distractions.
   To improve focus, memory, and further calm your nervous system, add in a cross-lateral (CL) exercise as you breathe.

CL exercises improve communication between your left and right-hemispheres. For instance, assuming you're like me and cannot juggle, try alternately touching your left thumb to your right forefinger, then right thumb to left forefinger, all while breathing slowly and deeply.

If you need a major physiological reset, take 30 seconds to stand up and march while alternately touching your right hand to left knee, then your left hand to your right knee. Extra credit if you teach your children to do these exercises when they feel a surge of cortisol from frustration or find it difficult to concentrate on the task at hand.

2. **ID Your MVPs.** Identify your Most Valued Priorities (MVPs). When your time and attention is stretched paper-thin, understanding your priorities is vital to maintaining your sanity. Ask yourself, what are my MVPs at this point in my life?

For example: family cohesion, physical health and financial security. When our family agreed to join the touring company for a Broadway show called *School of Rock,* I had no idea what to expect. However, I knew I wanted to travel, homeschool my boys, and escape the boredom I felt from the never-ending daily duties of my homelife. I was clear and honest with myself about my MVPs.

We ultimately traveled through 57 cities and out-schooled across the U.S. and Canada. LA traffic and trips to the market were replaced by meeting an astronaut, river rafting in Colorado, climbing through caves in Kentucky, snorkeling in the Florida Keys and exploring countless science, cultural, and art museums.

3. **Adapt.** Notice what's working well and give yourself permission to change what's not working well. Most successful business leaders find it second nature to adapt to shifts in their industry, learn from past mistakes, acknowledge market trends and make the necessary adjustments to maximize benefits and minimize risk. However, most rarely apply the same approach to their families or homelife.

Children vary greatly in personality and ability. They change over time, and family dynamics shift as well. The best way to treat your children *fairly* is to treat them differently, because they are, in fact, different people. Addressing all of your children in the same way, with the same rules, schedules, and expectations will only serve to limit their potential and maximize their frustration.

The Second Key: Clear Up Your Communication

How we speak and listen to the people in our world can make or break our relationships. Assuming you value your relationships with your loved ones more than your speaking engagements, then try these three tricks to Clear Up Your Communication:

1. **80% Positive.** Spend most of your time and energy focused on the positive. When speaking to your family, acknowledge what's working well MORE than you talk about what isn't working.

This is not a typical practice for most. Humans are wired to pay more attention to danger and threats in our environment. Purposely focusing on the positive allows you a more accurate perspective of reality, draws more positivity into your life, and frankly just makes you feel better.

2. **Team Up.** Invite your kids to be part of the team. Explain to them what you're working on, whom it's helping, and why it's important to you. When children understand what you're up to and how they can help, they feel empowered and respected rather than feeling like a mere annoyance.
3. **Thank You and I'm Sorry.** Verbally acknowledging what you appreciate about your children or their actions yields incredible results. Do it often, directly and genuinely. Giving a small and specific thank you works better than vague appreciation. For instance, "Thank you for loading the dirty dishes in the dishwasher while I put your sister to bed!" is more effective than "Thanks for your help!"

Apologies are best when they're done with vulnerability and honesty. Remember, there's no statute of limitations on an apology. If a long-lost friend called out of the blue to apologize for a wrongdoing, it would feel good, right?

Imagine how it might feel to receive a genuine apology from a loved one, even if it's been weeks since they made that snarky comment. If it's still on your mind, it's likely on theirs as well. Apologize to your children and you may see them apologize to one another more easily and more often.

The Third Key: Practice Purposeful Parenting

1. **Eisenhower at Home.** As business leaders, you cannot possibly do everything yourself. Use Eisenhower's Matrix to save yourself: Delete, Delegate, Delay, or Do It. While many of you likely practice this at work, you can also apply the principle at home.

Which tasks are neither important nor urgent? (Delete.) Which are urgent but not as important? (Delegate.) Important but not urgent? (Delay.) What you're left with is then both urgent and important to you. (Do It.)

Note: When delegating, I highly recommend you don't ask your children to share or split a task. They'll feel a sense of pride for accomplishing a full chore on their own and you'll avoid hearing, "But I did more work than he did!" I also find it more effective to do one of your own chores along-side them. Speak your appreciation then call grandma later (in front of the kids) and mention what a fabulous team of helpers you have!

Bigger Note: Don't Delegate a Trigger. A trigger is a task or job that will drive you crazy if done incorrectly, too late or not at all. Knowing yourself and understanding your personal triggers will save you from unwittingly delegating a task that will only end up annoying you when it's not done *right.*

2. **Interception Breaks.** If you're trying to work while the kids are doing virtual school - or if they're in the house at all - check in on them BEFORE they have a chance to come and find you. When you have a natural break, hop up and check in on each child in your family. This will result in fewer interruptions to your workflow,

allowing you to work much more efficiently. Children tend to feel more valued and are less likely to interrupt you when you seek them out instead of the other way around.

3. **SWEET Kids.** Behavior issues, irritability, sibling rivalry and difficulty with concentration will improve when children SWEET: Sleep, drink Water, Exercise, Eat and Take breaks.

Not sleeping well or not sleeping enough can affect kids, and adults, in a major way. Like you, they might be more mentally alert first thing in the morning or very late at night. If your child is getting enough sleep and doing their school work when they are most mentally alert, they'll be much more efficient and much less frustrated throughout the day.

Exercise. Although we all need to move our bodies, children need it even more than adults. Taking breaks throughout the day for children to move and oxygenate their blood will refuel their minds, increase emotional stability and improve physical health.

Drinking enough water and eating healthy foods throughout the day will help children stabilize their blood sugar levels, leaving them more receptive to learning, and less *hangry* or lethargic.

Take a break when you realize you've spent too much time on the computer or focused too long on the same task. Facilitating kid breaks throughout the day and modeling this skill yourself will serve both you and your children.

It may not be easy, but the tools are simple. Improving your mindset, communication and parenting will help you grow your business in a positive direction without losing your mind or your family in the process.

Even better, you may find yourself feeling more deeply connected to your family, more appreciative of your relationships, and more joyful, both at work and at home.

About Amber Trueblood

Amber Trueblood, MBA, LMFT is an author, speaker, podcaster, and mother of four sons. Through her interviews, workshops, the Stretch Marks book and The Stretch Marks Podcast, Amber teaches her clients how to minimize parenting challenges so they can improve their mental health and emotional sanity.

Contact Amber Trueblood

Facebook: https://www.facebook.com/stretchmarks

Instagram:https://www.instagram.com/officialambertrueblood

Website: https://ambertrueblood.com

LinkedIn: https://www.linkedin.com/in/amber-trueblood-ma-mba-469843149

Three Case Studies – One Lesson

Bob Hayward

In March 2020, while our minds were fixed on surging death rates across the world and the apocalyptic scenes in hospitals, global financial markets came as close to a collapse as they have since September 2008. Never has the global economy suffered a shock of this scale – every country at the same time.

For Zappshelter, a family business in Scotland, the future was not clear. 16,793 km from a key supplier and with the industries they serve shutting down few, if any, of their prospects were going to spending £15,000 or more on a temporary fabric shelter – however great.

Standard risk management techniques posed the family with some immediate questions:

1. What is the worst that could happen? No income for 12 months
2. How do we cope if the worst happens? Calculating their cash reality meant that business survival was going to be a tough fight
3. How do we improve upon the worst case? While cutting

those costs not essential to survival and growth could reduce expenditure by 25% it was the income side of the equation that needed some serious thinking

4. How could we prevent the worst from happening? While the family were not going to stop the global crisis, they could ensure sales were made and income was generated.

First Protect

Whether pivoting in good times or bad, it is vital to firstly protect and preserve the current business. Cut costs not required for stability and growth. Cut the fat, not the bone and muscle you need to respond to the situation, pivot and grow. Prepare for the worst, plan, and work for the best.

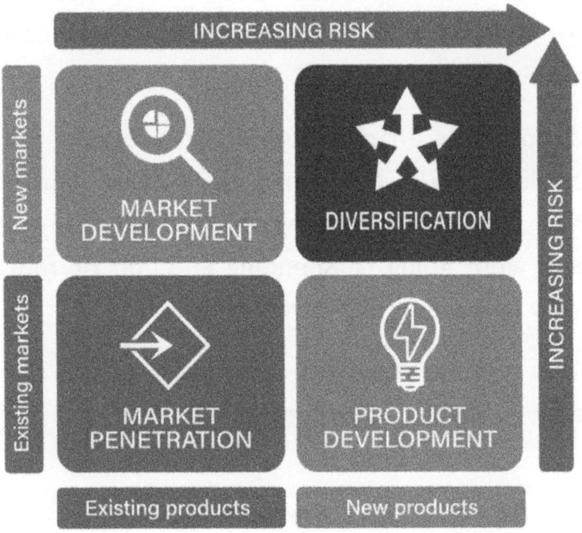

The Ansoff Matric Can Help Plan The Growth

- Could you sell more of your existing products to more prospects and customers in your current markets?
- Could you sell your existing products into new markets?
- Could you sell new products to your current clients?
- Could you sell new products into new markets? Tougher. What products? And which markets?

Adjust, Test And Learn

Few business advisors would recommend rushing into a seismic shift in business strategy. If your business must change directions it is vital that you get the pivot right. The second essential stage whether a 180-degree turn, or a less dramatic adjustment is to test and learn fast before you go large.

How can you get creative with what you have already got? Your current brand, purpose, values, capability, skills, network, clients, people, products? How can you pivot into an area of unmet need? Pivot into a high demand growing trend in a way that the competition has not?

Use SCAMPER to help you develop ideas. What can you:

- Substitute?
- Combine?
- Adapt?
- Modify?

- Put to another use?
- Eliminate?
- Reverse?

Once you have some ideas, test things out in a small way to preserve your cash, learn from real customer feedback, improve your offer and test again. Fail fast. Learn fast. Then go large.

Zappshelter's brand promise is to *Protect What Matters Most – People, Products and Profits* normally achieved by rapidly installed, very strong, temporary shelters that will last 25 years. Could these shelters be used to support the national cause? Yes, every virus testing station would need small temporary shelters that could protect the testing team from the inevitable British weather.

Within a week Zappshelter Air and other variants were created, along with a new UK/EU supply chain, adding the NHS and the MOD as clients to those in Construction, Aggregates and Waste. Extending a product range can be a quick and profitable pivot, leveraging your current brand, capability, knowledge, and network. Current customers often take up the new product rapidly as they trust you while also introducing you to additional markets.

Please do not underestimate how much thought and work is required to develop and test new products and gear up a new supply chain. Whether you attempt to do it in six months, six weeks, or six days it takes the same amount of effort.

So, if you intend to do it fast you will not get a lot of sleep.

In good times and bad the competition is likely to follow you, push you to be better, to be different. In a crisis some people rush to the bottom of the price spectrum out of fear or stupidity, be careful. Sales are vanity, profit is sanity. Especially in a crisis time you need a healthy margin. Sell on value not price. Even in tough times people know the difference between the two.

Bring The Future Into The Present And Do Something About It Now

The third essential stage is to keep the creative process going. While business has always been about live research and development, many businesses hit one big idea and then pursue it relentlessly to the exclusion of all else. A shock to the business ecosystem like a Global crisis brings with it the reminder of the need for constant R&D. Without innovation the world will overtake you at some point. New product and service development should never stop. While there is always a tension between changing too often or too fast, there is a massive problem with becoming complacent.

Zappshelter did not stop with the product extension pivot. At the same time, they had been working on a new product for their old and newly acquired markets.

What other products would fit the brand promise. To protect what matters most and serve the national interest? While a vaccine might be nice such a thing is not within the capability of many. Cleaning and sanitizing surfaces and equipment was a high demand and increasing trend. Even in lockdown, it was obvious we could not all stay at home forever. Some industries had to continue despite the lockdown, like food production and logistics so sanitizing vehicles, manufacturing equipment and in fact almost any surface people at work touched was required.

Welcome Zapptizer. All the separate elements of a new product or service do NOT have to be new themselves. Often blending elements previously only available separately can create something new. Sometimes transferring technology from one industry into another creates a fresh application.

Zapptizer was created with that approach. Take a proven, effective disinfecting, cleansing sanitizer, put it with a proven inert propellant in a high-pressure industrial sized canister and you have something the market loves. Now even the most difficult-to-reach areas on manufacturing equipment, in an ambulance, or in a welfare cabin can be treated fast and effectively.

The initial test marketing got a great response and customer feedback was very strong, so they put increasing amounts of time and effort behind marketing the product. While serving their old and newly acquired markets, Zapptizer also added Commercial, Hospitality and Education and has been a huge success. Still within the brand promise, still the same high quality, robust and long-lasting proposition, still with the same marketing, selling and customer service skills, still with a determination to protect and build their reputation but with different knowledge, a different supply chain and a different business model.

What About The Cash?

Payment upfront is significant enabler of growth. If you find a product that can meet a national need, how are you going to fund it? Your supply chain will need paying. More businesses run out of cash trying to grow than is realised. Cash up front is a game changer. Now you have cash in your bank account for 30 to 60 days before you must pay it to your suppliers. Now you can scale your business in line with what the market demands so long as your supply chain can keep up.

Zappshelter is a Capital expenditure item and requires a significant investment, Director's approval, purchase orders and payment terms. Zapptizer is a consumable, within most manager's expenditure limits and can be bought on a credit card. They did more than create a new product, in that very product was the cashflow to fund the growth.

Pivot Processes Too

What about a second-hand premium car dealership in the middle of nowhere?

When the 2020 crisis hit most car dealers, new or used, went into lockdown, furloughed their staff, and hoped the crisis did not last longer than their cash reserves. Not Steve Rogers, Director at Maundrell. From converted farm buildings on Blandys Farm in Letcombe Regis Oxfordshire, so truly in the middle of nowhere, he decided to pivot. Not what Maundrell excel at, exceptional professionalism and the highest quality pre-owned specialist cars. No, that remains sacrosanct. They pivoted how they sold.

Are you going to buy a £120,000 Ferrari or a £40,000 Porsche without seeing it? Prior to lockdown people would insist on driving to Blandys Farm to see a car. That could take 30 minutes or three hours depending where they lived. But there was nothing else anyone could do, if they wanted to see the car, was there? Well 360-degree spin cameras and viewing technology existed before the pandemic, it is simply that people felt it was not for them. They preferred to travel and see the car in person. Now under lockdown conditions the impressive immersive virtual tour of the car becomes the easiest and most accessible way to fulfil the ambition to own something special.

Before the pandemic, every car salesperson wants to conduct an all-important accompanied demonstration drive. During that 30-minute test drive the salesperson finds out your every need and dream. This is where most car sales are made, with you behind the wheel. Sorry Mr Car Dealer, during lockdown you cannot be that close to someone who does not live with you. Enter one of the eldest sales techniques in the sales mastery playbook. The puppy dog close. Leave us with your car, and some relevant insurance, and take your dream car home. It is clean and sanitised. We do not have to be any closer than two metres while swapping cars. Have the beauty for a week.

Now you might not have a salesperson beside you as you drive around familiar streets and your neighbours watch you enviously through their windows but come on. If that dream you saw on the 360-video tour matches your experience it is going to be incredibly hard, if not impossible to say no. Would you drive all the way back to Letcombe Regis to pick up a car you no longer want?

The combination of available technology with a creative approach to the sales process is all it took to pivot this car dealership, with huge success. While most of that industry simply stopped trading Steve turn an inconvenience into a brilliant new service.

What Happens To The Cleaner?

One way many businesses had to change direction was enabling staff to work from home. This has the potential to significantly improve employee engagement and productivity when done well. It also has the potential to cut costs significantly by reducing a huge cost. Office rent for many businesses is the second biggest cost after staff. What if you eliminated that cost all together? What could you do with the extra money? Take on more staff? Increase marketing spend?

One Consulting Firm in Oxford UK decided to do just. They decided to make working from home permanent. Exciting for the Consultants and Partners but what about the Cleaner. If you have negotiated the end of your lease and handed the keys back, you do not need a Cleaner. After 21 years one office cleaner was to be made redundant.

Enter Helen Lawrence, the Firm's HR Adviser.

How can you pivot in this situation? Can you find something better than following the traditional path? Whatever the Consulting Firm did they were legally obliged to pay the Cleaner a family substantial payoff after 21 years. When you look pragmatically at this situation there are some highly paid Consultants working from home. They are working well and working long hours. Those homes, just like the office did, need cleaning. How about offering the Cleaner a chance to set up a Cleaning Business with all the Consultants as the first set of clients? Now instead of making someone redundant, damaging their self-esteem, destabilising their lifestyle, and adding to the unemployment statistics they have created a bright new future for that Cleaner and made life easier for their staff. Happy staff are generally more productive. The business has significantly reduced costs and is immediately more profitable. This simple pivot should enable growth.

Summary

Pivoting each of these businesses required one thing. A change in thinking.

Their aim was to find a different answer to the problem that confronted them. A solution that solved the whole dilemma, for everyone, not just part of it. Something that created new value from existing assets, reduced costs, and increased flexibility. Turned an inconvenience into a new service. Finding a new way to deliver value. Shifting to a radically faster, better, cheaper supply chain, or monetizing differently with payment up front.

It is your thinking that pivots.

Good luck or bad luck it is how you think differently that changes your response and therefore the outcome.

About Bob Hayward

Bob Hayward, a Christian, a father to four, grandad to five (so far) and a Spurs fan; if you can cope with those facts then you will get on well with him.

He is a catalyst for change to those who want a business breakthrough, a best-selling author and popular international speaker. Having started seven businesses, and is still running two, he now loves using his experience and the skills developed along the way to make growth happen for others - sometimes as a Non-Executive Director, or a Growth Consultant or as a Senior Executive Coach.

He has designed and delivered numerous mission-critical internal communication initiatives, employee engagement projects and skill development programmes for companies like Vodafone, BMW, and Skype. Feedback on his work is high in both levels of delegate satisfaction and of tangible business improvements.

Bob has previously co-authored three Amazon Best Sellers:

- Persuade: How to persuade anyone about anything
- Remote Working: How to effectively and efficiently work from home in challenging times
- Fit for Purpose Leadership #6

Contact Bob Hayward

https://www.linkedin.com/in/bobhayward

Read More From Bob:

https://www.bemoreeffective.com/blog

https://twitter.com/bobhayward

https://www.amazon.co.uk/Robert-Hayward

To 'Pivot And Grow' Is To Succeed – In Life And Business

Tammy Banks

The term *Pivot* has become popular since the pandemic, maybe because we were all on the same *coronacoaster*, pivoting at the same time but what I've learned over the years is that life is a series of pivots. There are always defining moments in everyone's life where you have an opportunity to continue as you are or to need to *pivot and grow* to survive. These are forks in the road. One path means stagnation and being left behind. It means nothing ever changes.

Many people choose this path but really, it's a life of survival at best. The other path means evolving and adapting to thrive. It means embracing the opportunities that come your way, even if inside you feel afraid and unsure about whether you can rise to the challenge. It sets you on the path to success.

If you had told me when I was 15 that I would be where I am now, running my own successful company, working in Parliament, happily married with two children, I probably wouldn't have believed you.

You see, I was born into a cycle of harm and abuse. My childhood was chaotic to say the least and I dropped out of school and found myself homeless at 15 years of age. At the time I wouldn't have seen that as a pivot, but looking back I can see that my life has been a series of twists and turns, each one needing me to chose to *pivot and grow* or not.

Each one has helped me become the person I am today.

Sometimes we get so caught up in surviving from one day to the next that we can't see beyond that. This is true in both our business and personal life. I spent three years homeless and made many wrong choices along the way. I was lucky that a frontline professional gave me the opportunity to transform my life she helped me look to the future and not be overwhelmed by daily activities. I wouldn't want to experience this time in my life again, but equally, I wouldn't want to change it. It's part of who I am and to wish it away would mean wishing I was a different person.

It's perhaps not surprising that I chose to work in the Criminal Justice and Social Care sector on leaving university. I was drawn to working with homeless people, people in prison and charitable organisations.

I was driven, and passionate about helping people to escape from the cycle of harm and abuse so that they could live fulfilling lives. I took on the most challenging cases and worked with them to help them to transform their lives. I worked my way up into management roles and eventually became the CEO of a charity working to prevent sexual abuse.

By this point I realised my mission. To interrupt the generational cycle of abuse where possible.

However, I was continually frustrated because I was working in a sector where case-loads are increasing, frontline workers are burning out and having been there, I knew that every decision impacts lives. I had to think creatively for a solution that would cost organisations no more time or money than they were already spending.

So, I pivoted again. With my friend Faye Fox, I started to develop and deliver training courses delivered by people with experience of the issue and the sector. My belief was that if we could influence from the ground up through training, we could help make a positive impact on a larger number of frontline professionals, the people in the position to transform the lives of the most complex and/or vulnerable.

We have delivered thousands of courses for amazing organisations, our trainers deliver a huge range of safeguarding related subjects.

I love that our training has the power to transform lives, not only of the delegates but also the service users – complex and vulnerable people.

However, I still wanted to change things on a bigger scale so I pivoted again taking all my experience, from the ground up and became a Lay Member for the House of Commons' Committee on Standards, assessing and adjudicating complaints referred by the Commissioner and assisting with the development of new Codes of Conduct for MPs. This provides me with the opportunity to influence things at a strategic and political level. Yet I remain committed to influencing things at an operational level too because the frontline workers are the people who engage with disadvantaged people very day.

The Pivoting continued as we recognised our methodology 'Training 4 Influence' was applicable to any training subject, in every sector and we started to share it through our train the trainer course. Helping people wider than Taye to transform their training sessions so they build emotional resilience, inspire and engage every delegate.

However, my most recent pivot and the one that has me reflecting occurred as a result of the pandemic. Overnight, like many businesses, we faced the loss of training bookings due to physical distancing and lockdown measures. That could have wiped out our entire business. Through tears, I asked one of the team to research video conferencing platforms so that we could take our business online quickly and efficiently. However, I didn't want to compromise on the quality of delivery or to produce static and disengaging e-learning. I wanted it to be engaging and interactive and delivered by an operational expert.

So we had a lot of learning to do.

We've managed to produce live online learning that is fun, informative and active – live online training that delivers the high standards our methodology insists upon. and as a result, we are thriving and showing other people how they can deliver in this way.

Going forward we plan now to offer a blended approach to learning – another pivot. I'm so proud of this Pivot that although my book *Transform Your Training* was already with the publishers I recalled it to add another chapter specifically about using our methodology during live online training.

I love my life and although it hasn't been easy I truly believe one of the keys to my success has been the ability to pivot and grow continually. It's a skill to be able to recognise opportunities when they present themselves. Sometimes they will be obvious, and you'll want to grab them with both hands. At other times you'll face setbacks and disappointments and need to be able to have the vision to see that if one door is closing on you, it means another is opening elsewhere. There will be other times when you won't recognise what has happened until after the event. I often haven't.

Sometimes you'll face these moments alone. At other times you'll have people to help you navigate them. When I was young and homeless frontline professionals helped me to pivot to change my life and, as a result, I'm now fulfilled, contributing to society and making a positive impact. Changing paths has meant that my children will never experience the devastation I did. They already believe the world is full of possibilities and that they are loved beyond measure. Recently my helpers have ranged from my immediate family, the team at Taye training and to the wonderful business communities I am part of.

It's about staying connected to your values and your *why*. When you're clear about your values and you're *why* for doing what you do, they act as a form of guiding light. When you come to a fork in the road, tuning in to what matters to you and making decisions based on it will move you forward in the right direction even if you don't initially see it. That might mean turning down an opportunity that doesn't feel right, to make space for a better opportunity to come along later. Pivoting means facing your fears and taking bold steps. It means believing in yourself and those around you. It means trusting that you CAN do this. It means drawing on the strength and resources you already have within you and acquiring new skills, knowledge and experience.

Through life, personal and business, it's important to keep moving forward. You might pivot and take a step back, but your eyes need to stay on the way ahead so that you can recognise the next leap forward. It's about resilience, strength of character, determination and self-belief.

About Tammy Banks

Tammy's personal history, academic achievements and work experience have driven her to champion the importance of effective, achievable solutions to prevent abuse and poverty. Tammy leads with passion and commitment, recognising the importance of advocating for change while delivering operational solutions.

Tammy is co-director of Taye Training and Author of the book *Transform Your Training* written to share the *Training 4 Influence* methodology.

Tammy's TEDx talk *The importance of being kind* can be found on YouTube.

Contact Tammy Banks

You can connect with Tammy on social media:

Twitter @tammybanksy @training4Influ I @Tayetraining

LinkedIn Tammy Banks

Instagram Training4Influence TayeTraining

Facebook Training 4 Influence Taye Training Tammy Banks

Or find out more about the training methodology

www.training4influence.co.uk

or Taye Training *www.tayetraining.org.uk*

Double Your Tender Win-Rate: A Recipe Of Seven Ingredients

Scott Keyser

Most contests typically follow a 2-step sequence: an informal pre-contest phase, and the contest itself.

In a public auction, punters can inspect the lots at their leisure. But when the auctioneer launches the auction with the opening price for lot one, the game has moved into the contest phase, with strict rules of engagement.

In ancient Rome, senators wanting to bet on a gladiator could inspect and speak to the gladiators beforehand. But the moment the gladiators stepped onto the sand of the arena and the war trumpet sounded, the contest had begun.

And punters wanting to bet on a horserace can view the horses close-up as their grooms lead them around the paddock pre-race. But when the starter's gun goes off and the horses fly out of their stalls, the contest has begun.

So it is in competitive tendering.

The moment the buyer publishes the Request for Proposal/

Invitation To Tender (RFP/ITT), the process has moved into the contest phase, where bidders must play by the buyer's (often onerous) rules and time-scales. Here, access to decision-makers is rare, especially in public sector tenders. Like a watershed in a river system, the publishing of the RFP/ ITT is a clear dividing line between the two distinct phases of the contest.

Which is why it's odd that so few bidders use the pre-contest phase to get to know and build trust with the buyer. You'd hardly bid for a property or a car without visiting it first or kicking its tyres, would you?

That's why, of the seven ingredients of my (now not so secret) Secret Sauce spanning the entire bidding process end-to-end and that this article covers, five, arguably six, are added to the BD mix pre-tender.

This is front-loaded BD; it offers a proactive alternative to the reactivity of slavishly responding to a buyer's invitation to tender. World-class bidders have all seven ingredients in their BD sauce.

Ingredient #1: Nail Your Value Proposition

Your value proposition (VP) is your distinctive offer of value to a particular market. It's what you do and how you communicate to that market what you do.

A VP typically contains seven Ps, of which the most neglected are People, Pain, Promise and Price. In other words, who do you work with, what are their typical pain points, what are the benefits to them of removing that pain, and what do you charge to do so?

For example, I work with Heads of Bids/BD in professional services (People) whose tender win-rate is lower than they would like (Pain). I help them to install the skills, mindset, processes and practices needed to double their tender win-rate (Promise), for which I charge £XXX (Price).

The clarity, confidence and certainty that come from nailing your VP will shine through your bids.

Ingredient #2: Bind The Golden Thread Of Pain-Value-Price

What undermines most bids is a poor understanding of each individual buyer's pain points.

If your understanding of this and the value to them of removing that pain is poor, the price/value relationship breaks down. The buyers won't see the inter-dependence between the value they get and the price you charge to deliver that value.

And your proposed solution risks making no sense. Your understanding of their pain is the raw material you use to tailor your response to their particular needs; it's the launchpad for your solution. If they can't see how your solution matches their pain, you have a dysfunctional proposal.

The intimate relationship between each buyer's Pain points, the Value to them of removing that pain and the Price you'll charge to do so is what I call The (P-V-P) Golden Thread.

The Golden Thread unifies great bids. It starts with a thorough understanding of each buyer's pain.

Ingredient #3: Build A 90% Bid Library

You should be able to predict 90% of the questions that a buyer will ask you in a bid, eg:

- Industry experience ('track-record')
- Relevant case studies
- Industry awards
- Financial performance
- ESG (Environmental, Social & Governance) credentials
- Method statement (how you do what you do)
- Policies & procedures (eg health & safety, modern slavery)
- CVs/profiles of senior managers, directors and the Board
- References/referees
- Standard fees/rate card/price list

Doesn't it make sense to have a library of pre-approved responses to these routine questions? Even if you don't use them verbatim in your response, at least you have the raw material to adapt to each bid. You're not having to re-invent the wheel.

The obvious benefit of a 90% bid library is that it frees you and your team to focus on the vital 10% that you customise to the buyer's specific situation — like binding The Golden Thread of Pain, Value and Price.

Ingredient #4: Streamline Your Bid Process

One way to ensure your bid process runs smoothly is to treat each bid like a project.

Bids have an output (the bid document or pitch); a desired outcome (contract award); prescribed time-scales; internal milestones (pre-qualification, kick-off and review meetings, document drafts, rehearsals, presentation etc); a scope (defined by the spec and the RFP/ITT), and require close stakeholder management (the bid team and other contributors to the bid).

Most of my bid process audits, however, find the opposite: a loosely agreed process that service lines pay lip-service to, but which in practice they don't follow; they do their own thing.

The risk of not following an agreed process with clear milestones, roles and accountabilities is that things get missed or half-done: the vital pre-qualification meeting either doesn't happen or the decision to bid is made on the fly; the response is slow, with resources mobilised only when the deadline looms; the kick-off meeting — which should launch the internal bid process and set the tone for the whole response — gets too little focus from senior stakeholders.

The time-scales of most tenders are tight. Don't make it worse by bidding by the seat of your pants. It'll show up in your win-rate.

Ingredient #5: Develop World-Class Bidding Skills

This includes asking questions that get the buyers talking; building rapport; writing like a god; pitching like a pro.

Your questions must get each buyer talking at length about their pain points. Get them to articulate in their own words the gap between where they are now and where they want to be. That value gap is what your solution must fill.

We build rapport through questions. When our questions land and make the buyers think differently about their business and their pain, a rapport forms.

As for writing, your bid response needs to be well structured, clear, concise and compelling. Space precludes me from saying much about this here, other than to issue a challenge: every single page of your bid must either be about the buyer or add value to them in some way.

When it comes to the pitch, planning, preparing and rehearsing it are vital, as well as prepping the crucial Q&A, which accounts for 75% of the buyers' vote.

There is, however, one thing that transcends all the above, and it's not to do with skills; it's to do with intention.

In my experience, if the buyer senses that your genuine intention is to add value to their business, they'll be majorly forgiving of minor typos, un-slick presenting or social awkwardness.

Ingredient #6: Pre-qualify Every Major Opportunity

If you want to double your tender win-rate, pre-qualify every opportunity. You'll end up bidding for fewer opportunities but winning more of them. And the ones you do win will be the ones you really want.

That's what we did at Ernst & Young.

We (National Proposals) convinced the partners to pre-qualify. Instead of bidding for anything that moved, they became much choosier about the opportunities available, committing heftier resources to the ones they bid for.

To pre-qualify, look at four abilities:

1. **Is it winnable?** This is to do with the quality of your relationship with the buyers. Do they already know, like and trust you? If they don't, you're on the back foot.
2. **Is it desirable?** This is about relevance to your core business, and your motivation. If the opportunity is in your 'sweet spot', you'll be gagging to bid.
3. **Is it deliverable?** You may win the bid, but do you have the capability and the capacity to deliver against the spec? If it's going to be a stretch for your business, think twice.
4. **Is it profitable?** Fairly obvious, but there's no point bidding for a contract with tiny margins in the hope of making up for it later through change orders or scope adjustments.

Ingredient #7: Get Buyer Feedback Post-Award

This is the only ingredient in the Secret Sauce that gets added post-tender.

Win, lose or draw, you must research every major proposal once the client has made their decision. Otherwise, how will you learn and improve? Your goal is to get candid feedback, to understand how your bid influenced their decision.

To ensure candour, use a third party. At Ernst & Young we briefed an independent research company to interview the client after every major submission. Most clients gave an hour and the researcher posed our questions, recorded and transcribed the interview, and summarised the findings.

We learnt what we did well, what to do differently next time and what to stop doing altogether. It gave us the ammunition and authority to spread the word of proposals best practice throughout the firm, as well as give the team in question feedback they could apply to their next bid.

It was gold dust.

End-Note

You may be using one of the above ingredients or all seven. Your BD sauce may be a rich mix or a thin gruel. Either way, improving each ingredient by a mere 5% will result in a huge overall impact on your tendering win-rate.

About Scott Keyser

Scott is The Writing Guy, a twice-published bid writer, consultant and trainer who helps professional services firms to write Human and double their tender win-rate. He helps clients produce world-class bids by binding what he calls *The Golden Thread* between the buyer's pain, the value to them of removing that pain, and the price the bidder will charge to do so.

Scott's proudest achievements are:

- Helping Ernst & Young double its tender win-rate
- Taking an international consultancy's tender win-rate from 14% to 71%
- Delivering his bid writing workshop to 100s of BD professionals around the world, averaging 90% satisfaction over 16 years
- Training staff of *The Economist* in writing skills for a decade
- Having two books published: *Winner Takes All* and *rhetorica* ® *- a toolkit of 21 everyday writing techniques*

Contact Scott Keyser

www.writeforresults.com

scott@writeforresults.com

Connecting The Head And Heart Pivoting To Exceptional Online Business Events

Lorna Reeves

"I see webinars and online workshops all the time and they simply won't work for my business and clients...."

This is a conversation I was having for the umpteenth time this week. I was speaking with an incredible business owner who has an amazing offer, delivering training and development in an immersive way in the face-to-face world. Their feedback was always exemplary, and their clients went on to be disciples and hugely successful in their own right – thanks to the knowledge and skills they learned in the room with our business owner.

However, the world has taken a giant leap forward. We have all experienced there is a perceptible shift in the way we all want to work and have experiences now. We have, in typical human fashion, adapted and now think twice about travelling hours to a big city for a training/ learning event.

Companies and businesses are looking at their bottom lines and really considering, *Do we need to be paying for travel and accommodation for our trainers? Plus subsistence for the delegates? We have saved so much in venue and food costs in the first quarter of 2020, can we use this elsewhere?*

Quite right that businesses are having these conversations and we, as service-based businesses need to ensure we are adapting quickly and effectively to maintain stellar delivery and results to our clients in a way that now serves their changed needs.

In March 2020, when European governments, one by one, announced lockdowns I knew that my world was about the change forever. From having a company and team based around delivering international immersive, interactive and engaging face-to-face business events for our clients; being booked for the next 12 months – my concern was real and immediate. I turned to my wife and said, "I need to shift, pivot, reinvent fast, or we'll be sunk!"

Three days later, with very little sleep and I had converted our clients to delivery of their events in the virtual space. Enabling them to deliver engaging workshops, utilising the ever-changing and developing technology around us.

Moving your product from in-person to online delivery is not as simple as taking your session outline, using your pre-written presentation, and delivering the same thing in Zoom. 4D experiences rarely translate directly to online and often come across as flat lectures. We know that humans learn via many methods and media, none more potent than immersive experience and coupling that with emotional engagement. With surveys reporting that 47% of employees expect to maintain at least some of their remote working, and employers noticing a 45% increase in productivity – we can be sure that accessing your audience in the virtual realm is here to stay.

Where To Start?

When designing an online workshop, seminar, conference or session, I invite my clients to go back to the *Why?* It really is the Vision part of our E.V.E.N.T.S process but works well to transition here. Perhaps ask yourself:

- What am I looking to achieve from this Event (session/ workshop etc)?
- What do I want my participants to walk away knowing?
- How did I want my participants to feel?
- What is the mood we are trying to create?
- Do we want people to buy/ reflect/ learn?

When you have this part of your vision clear, next we need to think about the wish list; in the ideal world where anything is possible online, what tools would you like to bring from in-person events to this virtual space?

Here is where you need to think *interactivity*, it might sound impossible, but you might be surprised as to the tech possibilities.

Here are some ideas:

- Flip charts
- Presentations with music and video
- Group working and plenary discussion
- Quiet reflective periods
- Workshopping/ practicing of skills
- World café – the ability for participants to travel from room to room and choose their conversation or the person they listen to.
- Multi-room experiences with multi sessions running at the same time.
- Do you want them to experience a place, task or role? Think virtual reality

Do not think small here! Let your creativity run free and really stand a moment in your participants' shoes. The difference between a good online event and a phenomenal one is user experience, thinking big here will set you apart.

Only with these two elements of your Vision clear can we move on.

Interaction

In the previous section, I have talked heavily as to increasing interaction and moving away from the *lecture* style webinar. To be clear, the term Webinar for most platforms should read *Broadcast*. Webinars are generally a single flow of information from you, the speaker, to the audience.

You don't see the audience's face or hear their voice apart from chat (generally speaking). The function of *Meetings* tend to be more for the interactive space. But this is not set in stone.

We live in a world now with so many streams of information available and flying at us continually, that very few people now learn or have the capacity to learn in a lecture-style format, particularly in the online space, there are too many distractions; emails pinging, phone ringing, children singing, dogs whining (you get the idea). I have experienced that there is nothing more significant in the way in which participants learn than the emotion and mood they experience in a session, in-person or online.

Many have completed work in this field, Vuilleumier, 2005 discusses emotions and attention, Phelps, 2004, and Um et al., 2012, discuss emotional and impact on learning and memory, to name a few. We now know that knowledge collected, processed and retained in a learning session is significantly impacted by mood and emotion, the time that we retain the information can be affected by as much as 75% depending on emotion of the learner.

We also know that boredom and distraction, shifts our participants from the mood and emotion bubble we create in our sessions and that the value of it is lost as soon as they disengage. This is the reason that creating an interactive, immersive session – even in the online space is so important.

Keeping the participants' attention in the room and keeping people connected to you and your content ensures information and experience is processed quickly and imbedded as permanent learning.

Choosing Your Platform

Now you have your wish list of tools and your vision you can consider your platform. By building your session this way, means you approach the online event from the participants' experience rather than building a session built on limitations of the tech available to you.

There are so many platforms to choose from and all have their pros and cons; Microsoft Teams – meeting or live, Google Meets – meeting or broadcast, Zoom – meeting or Webinar, HopOn, On24, ClickMeeting, GotoMeeting… and the list goes on with new software emerging every day.

Choose a platform or two together, to create the experience you want for your participants. You are not tied to one platform, one link. You can use multiples in tandem if you wish. For example, a conference might have three Zoom Webinars, three Zoom meetings and nine Breakout spaces within them, then a Virtual reality Networking meeting attached. There is nothing to stop you from recreating that *walk-around* feel in a virtual space.

Choose platforms that work for you and your comfort levels, as well as your online session design and your participants – utilise the free trials on all of these and get the know what they can do, how do you find them as a user? Then you can commit to a paid account should you need one.

User Experience

Lastly, when finalising your plans for your session, do revisit your *Why*. Creating a user experience and connecting this with how you want the participants to feel when they are in and when they leave your session will have the most impact on the next steps they take and the impression they are left with of you and your company.

When signing participants up, make sure your instructions are clear, exact and repetitive and available to view in many ways. A frustrated participant will arrive at your session in a negative mood, moods last far longer than emotions. A negative mood will severely hamper the learning taking place, the immersion, and the ability of the person to fully engage with you and your content and the perception of your session.

How Do You Ensure Participants Arrive With A 'Seeking' Mood And Emotions?

Ensure your joining instructions are clear, in word, diagram/images and potentially video for all learning types. Have a contingency for helping participants if they struggle to access your event. Have multiple buttons directing them to the correct links. If you have given instructions a couple of times and are not sure if it's enough – add them another time!

Participants will forgive hiccoughs and technical glitches if they know you are doing your best to make their journey as smooth as possible and recover quickly from any glitches. That said, always ensure you have help to deliver your online sessions.

It is hard work delivering, keeping your energy high to translate through a screen, roll your presentation and deliver your content. To try to attend to all your participants' needs and troubleshooting too, is a mammoth task.

Having someone who can *produce* your event for you and assist with those elements is a must and again ensures high level user-experiences, sets the mood, emotions and energy in your virtual space.

All these elements combined ensure your participants are engaged, immersed and fast-tracks you to landing your message well and consistently.

In short, to shift your delivery online:

- Start with your *Why*
- Think about your 'ideal' session
- Construct your Vision
- Always think interactively
- Then choose your delivery platform to suit
- Focus on user-experience to maximise immersion, emotion and engagement.

This formula will elevate your events, your products and your brand and will ensure you are showing up in your industry moving forward. Standing out in your industry and gaining your perfect clients sometimes means stepping off the curve of the *norm*.

Focusing on your participants rather than what you want to say will ensure your online events are exceptional, outstanding and pack a punch time after time.

References

- Phelps, E. A. (2004). Human emotion and memory: interactions of the amygdala and hippocampal complex. Curr. Opin. Neurobiol. 14, 198–202. doi: 10.1016/j.conb.2004.03.015
- PubMed Abstract | CrossRef Full Text | Google Scholar
- Um, E., Plass, J. L., Hayward, E. O., and Homer, B. D. (2012). Emotional design in multimedia learning. J. Educ. Psychol. 104, 485–498. doi: 10.1037/a0026609
- CrossRef Full Text | Google Scholar
- Vuilleumier, P. (2005). How brains beware: neural mechanisms of emotional attention. Trends Cogn. Sci. 9, 585–594. doi: 10.1016/j.tics.2005.10.011
- PubMed Abstract | CrossRef Full Text | Google Scholar

About Lorna Reeves

Lorna Reeves is a multi-award winning, business owner, speaker and author. After 15 years as a CSI in the Metropolitan Police, Lorna finished her career in Forensics, managing a team of 160, multi-million-pound contracts, 3000 cases annually, procurement, HR and negotiation. She took these skills and uses them in her business.

Lorna started her first business, MyOhMyWeddings with her passion and dedicated to supporting the LGBT+ community to create their perfect day without any limitations. Lorna is a force for change, driving and establishing a representation and a voice for the LGBTQ+ community in the wedding industry.

MyOhMy Events, Lorna's second business allows her to pursue her passion for creating experiential, game changing business events; elevating her clients' brands, in the campaign for no more boring conference spaces and lectures. Pivoting to online in March 2020 to triple turnover in ten days.

Now she and her team deliver seminars, workshops and multi-day conferences to clients globally.

Lorna's solution focussed, no-nonsense style ensures her client's events elevate their brand.

Contact Lorna Reeves

lorna@myohmyevents.com

www.myohmyevents.com

Instagram @myohmy_events

https://www.facebook.com/myohmyevents/

https://www.linkedin.com/in/o lorna-reeves-planner/

So, What Do You Do?

Robin Waite

That awkward moment when you get along to a networking meeting and someone asks you the dreaded question, "So, what do you DO?"

Most business owners get flustered and end up giving the unwitting recipient their job title before the conversation shifts gears into, "Have you travelled far?"

They exchange business cards, and both are left still wondering what the other person does.

Business owners do not always need to pivot to grow. They would simply be better off refining the core pillars of their business so that they are able to better articulate their value to prospective customers.

If you yourself are an entrepreneur, this will be as influential as a pivot. This is likely the first time someone has invited you to be super specific with your offer.

There are three core ingredients which go into building a niche offer: your **Market Niche**, your **Product Niche** and your **Pricing Niche.**

Most entrepreneurs fail at this because they are not specific about any of these three core pillars.

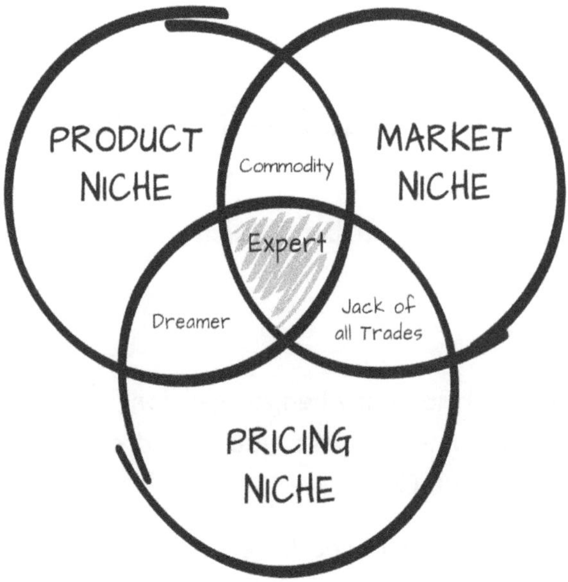

The Market Niche

The biggest bugbear I have with marketing is born out of asking entrepreneurs who their target market is, and then being given the answer, *SMEs!*

SME is NOT a target market. There are six million registered small businesses in the UK, and only 40,000 of them are considered large businesses (comprising 250+ employees).

Therefore, SME is not a target market, it is ALL the market.

The same entrepreneurs then wonder why they struggle with marketing and are constantly looking at innovative ways to reach new audiences.

Marketing has changed dramatically over the past 30 years thanks to the Internet.

When Facebook was founded in 2003 many of the marketing apps and platforms you take for granted now did not even exist. Many entrepreneurs spend their days pivoting from one platform to the next, spending very little time mastering the platform and finally give up stating, "This platform doesn't work for me."

These platforms are tools that we use in marketing and entrepreneurs seem to skip over the question, *Who is my perfect client and where do they hang out?* in favour of the next new shiny thing.

Why do entrepreneurs struggle so much with this question?

It's driven by a fear - the Fear of Missing Out (FOMO), *If I ONLY work with Beagle owners, am I not missing out on being able to train all of the dog breeds that are out there?*

No! There are millions of Beagles.

Here are three simple questions that you can ask yourself when identifying your ideal audience:

1. Who do I love working with the most?
2. Who do I get the best results for?
3. Who can afford to buy my products/services?

Make your answers as binary as possible. If your answer contains the words *kind of* i.e. *I kind of like working with...* then that audience is OUT!

Imagine you are walking into a networking meeting for

the first time and you must give your 60 second pitch. If you are an accountant, you likely start your pitch with, "Hi, I'm Dave/Trish/Sue. I'm an accountant and I work with SMEs…" whereas if you started it like this, "I work with *beauty therapists* who struggle with numbers…" The Beauty Therapists in the room will sit up and listen?

Be specific with who your ideal client avatar is. Super specific.

The Product Niche

How often have you asked someone what they can do for you and their reply is, *Anything you want!*

I would never buy from that person.

It means they are a jack of all trades and a master at none. We've seen them all before; the full-service marketing agency, the VA who'll run your entire business, the dog trainer who works with any person and their dog.

You are often left wondering what it is that person does for a living. The results seem *acceptable*. And their fees seem, *A little high for what they do.*

There is one way to know if this is you; when you pitch prospective clients, they will select from your services like it is an A La Carte menu. Often saying things like, *I don't think I need that.*

Take the Henry Ford approach, *You can have any colour you want, so long as it's black!*

When you are specific in your Product Niche there are very few questions left to be asked.

It is obvious what you do. If someone were to introduce you to a colleague they would do so swiftly and succinctly.

As an example, I hired a VA service which sources guest slots for Business Coaches on Top 100 Podcasts.

Did you notice I dropped the Market Niche in there, too?

There are millions of businesses out there, but this VA specifically works with Business Coaches. They offer a great service, hitting both Market and Product Niches. As a result they are reassuringly expensive.

You can see that if you occupy both Product and Market Niches but not a Pricing Niche then you are selling a Commodity.

The Pricing Niche

Ask any entrepreneur how they settled on their prices and they will likely reply, *I looked at my competition to see how much they were charging.*

Competitor research is a great idea; however, the mistake is assuming that your competition is right when it comes to pricing.

When you compare yourself to your competitor's prices you have three choices:

1. Be the cheapest - some entrepreneurs think that being the cheapest is how you attract new customers. They are left struggling, working all hours for customers who do not really get their value.

2. Middle of the road - they do not want to be the cheapest, but do not want to be the most expensive, assuming that being the most expensive it will put potential customers off.
3. The most expensive.

Imagine there are 20 people doing what you do in your local area. Only ONE entrepreneur can be the most expensive. Often the most expensive has been around for years, has the best reputation and gets the best results for their clients.

Let me reiterate that... they have been around for ages; they are the most expensive and YET they STILL GET CLIENTS.

It therefore makes sense to position yourself at the head of the market. Chances are if you are good at marketing and sales, then you will get top rate clients.

Where an entrepreneur has a Product and Pricing Niche but does not have a Market Niche, they become the *Dreamers*. Like the entrepreneurs you see on Dragon's Den where they overvalue their business and have no clients. The Dragons often tell them to stop throwing money at their idea.

Contrary to that, if an entrepreneur has a Market and Pricing Niche but not a Product Niche, prospective clients don't know what they REALLY do, results are unclear and they become the Jack if all Trades, saying, *Yes!* to everything. Ultimately stifling scalability.

In Summary

You may have spotted nailing your Product, Market and Pricing niche is not a pivot. There is no need to switch your marketing strategy or wildly change your product.

Instead I am suggesting you refine your Market Niche, so it is super specific.

Sell a super specific product; the one product where you get the BEST results for your customers.

And be the most expensive among your competition because someone has got to.

Case Studies

The Podcast VA - Virtual Assistants are ten-a-penny working for any business needing their help and doing any job from client enrolment to social media and inbox/diary management. They charge from $6/hr up to $40/hr.

At a recent VA Conference, we discussed the Market, Product and Pricing niches. The example we came up with was a Podcast Concierge Service for Business Coaches.

If a VA could find some Top 100 Podcasts for a business coach to guest on it could lead to dozens of enquiries and thousands in revenue.

We designed a pack of 10 podcast appearances for $2,500. It took on average just one hour to source and book each interview for their client.

That is nearly 10x their previous hourly rate.

The Dog Trainer - The Market Niche and Product Niche go together by narrowing down both niches based on a dog's breed.

A Dog Trainer specialising in Beagles has since gone on to grow a niche Facebook Group of 9,000 Beagle owners.

Originally thinking that this would narrow their audience, it did initially in the UK, but it opened her business up to Beagle owners worldwide.

Most dog trainers charge between £40-£90 for an initial consultation, but several trainers who have niched down on specific breeds charge as much as £820 per consultation.

The Accountancy Practice - Speak to most accountants and they will take on clients of all sizes in any industry

This Accountancy Practice, however, only worked with £1m tech companies who required help with Research and Development (R&D) Tax Credits.

Most small business compliance work yields between £1,200-£5,000 per annum, the typical R&D claim this Accountancy Practice worked on was £250,000 or more.

Their fee is a fixed percentage of 13% of the total claim. Meaning they can command fees of 5-10x the *average* accountancy client.

About Robin Waite

Robin Waite is Founder of Fearless Business and bestselling author of Online Business Startup and Take Your Shot.

After 12 years running a marketing agency, Waite Founded Fearless Business in 2016. Fearless Business is a business accelerator for Coaches, Consultants and Freelancers.

Contact Robin Waite

Websites: *https://robinwaite.com/* & *https://fearless.biz*

Twitter: *https://twitter.com/RobinMWaite*

Facebook: *https://facebook.com/RobinMWaite*

LinkedIn: *https://www.linkedin.com/in/Robinmwaite*

Online Business Startup: *http://www.amazon.co.uk/dp/B00W7LXGL0*

Take Your Shot: *https://www.amazon.co.uk/dp/B074679GZ6*

Pick A Lane!

Sammy Blindell

"If you are not leading, you are losing out and for every moment your ideal customers are investing in someone else, they are losing out too."

Sammy Blindell

You will only ever know of 1% of your impact in this world.

The likes and comments on your social media posts represent around 1% of the people who view your posts. Many others follow you, but you'll never know who they are.

The customers who take the time to thank you are only around 1% of those customers who are really grateful for the work you do. Many others are profoundly grateful, but you'll never know because they simply won't tell you.

Think about it for a moment ... you have already made such an enormous impact on so many people and yet you probably still feel like you aren't achieving enough. You still feel like there is so much to do, right?

You know you are here at this time in history to make a bigger difference. You feel the calling to do something greater, to make a bigger impact. Yet I'm guessing there's still part of you that feels like there is so much more you could and should be doing to achieve that impact faster.

The reality is that you must slow down to speed up.

This seems counter intuitive doesn't it? *If money loves momentum and success loves speed, how can slowing down accelerate the impact I make, Sammy?* I hear you say!

After building nine companies and supporting many thousands of small business owners around the world to build theirs, I know the most productive and efficient way to build your brand is to take a step back and pick a lane before you drive forward.

In just the last three months alone, millions of jobs have disappeared and hundreds of thousands of people started their own business as a Coach, Consultant, Trainer or Influencer to survive. I am in contact with around 57,000 business owners every week across our various channels and have received hundreds of worried messages asking for help. They are having to work three times harder now just to achieve the same level of income they had before lockdown. Competition has shot up and it's not just local or national competition anymore, your competition is now global.

Prior to the 2020 lockdown, you only had to think about competitors in your own industry. But now, with so many new businesses flooding the internet ready to serve on Zoom, you are competing with every other business owner on the planet for the same time, attention, budget, advertising, and eyeballs.

The reality is that it no longer matters how experienced you are, how many years you've been doing what you do or how long you've been in business. There are many thousands of fresh new start-up businesses who only need to learn how to brand themselves better than you to attract your dream customers and they'll be taking all of the business that could have been yours.

So, how do you brand yourself brilliantly and outpace any competition?

You create your *Fame Name* and get known 100% for just ONE THING.

Oh, and if you already have a Fame Name, now is a great time to check-in using the process I'm going to give you, to ensure it still represents the brand you are growing into, instead of who you are now.

Your Fame Name is a simple identifier of just three to four words that make it totally obvious to a stranger who you are, what you do and how you do it.

Perhaps you are thinking right now... *It's impossible to sum up everything I do in just three to four words.* However, once you know the process, I'm pretty sure you will flow straight through it.

Create your Fame Name by getting totally clear on your brand promise. To start, answer these three questions:

1. WHAT'S ONE THING you deliver for your customers 100% of the time?
2. WHAT'S ONE SERVICE you really want to be known for 100% of the time?

3. WHAT'S ONE RESULT you leave your customers with 100% of the time?

Ultimately, this is the basis of creating a great Fame Name that is catchy, memorable, and most importantly, repeatable. The challenge with you not having a Fame Name is that your business will be unidentifiable, unrecognisable, and therefore unsustainable.

Your brand is what other people say it is when you are not there. So if someone talks about you in a different way each time, you have no brand. You could have the best logo (branding) in the world, but if you don't have a consistently solid reputation (brand), you don't have a sustainable business. An inconsistent brand will create unconscious barriers between you and the customers you most want to serve.

"If your brand is inconsistent,
people will believe what you deliver is inconsistent."

Building a business without a brand is hard work and hard work is not sustainable for a long period of time. It leads to burnout and given this book is all about how to build a sustainable business, my mission as your Mentor in this chapter is to ensure you build a business you love, that gives you everything you want in life, along with plenty of time freedom so you don't burn out.

I know what it's like to burn out and it pains me to see thousands of business owners burning themselves out right now, selling their time for money, over-delivering, undercharging and chasing financial goals that lead to a *busy-mess* rather than a business.

Inconsistent brands create inconsistent trust and inconsistent cashflow. These three things lead you to working harder to make ends meet, stealing you away from the people who matter most to you. I never want you to experience the heartache that follows this kind of up and down lifestyle, because having almost had a heart attack age thirty-eight in 2013 whilst building my multi-million-pound branding agency, I know for sure that losing your health to business really isn't worth it.

I'm going to take you through the Fame Name process now. However, there's only so much I can do to help you achieve it within the 1800 words I have with you in this chapter! So, I've created you a 1 hour online training to go with this chapter that walks you through the personal branding process further, to help you understand the building blocks you need to put in place immediately to become the market leader in your industry - before someone else does.

Look out for the link at the end of this chapter.

Your Fame Name should be no more than 3 words (4 maximum). The more words you use, the more you give others to remember, so less is more with your Fame Name. It should be catchy, memorable, repeatable, and definitely shareable!

Here is the process for creating your Fame Name...

1. The first word is easy, because out of the three words you have to play with, your first word is THE!

2. The second word of your Fame Name should be WHAT YOU MOST WANT TO BE KNOWN FOR.

3. The third word of your Fame Name should be THE OUTCOME/RESULT YOUR CLIENTS RECEIVE.

Brand is what I most want to be known for and building their brand is what my clients receive, so The Brand Builder is perfect,

In May 2020, I published *The Law of Brand Attraction* book and featured 22 of my Brand Builders Club members in it, along with two of my dear friends from *The Secret*. I have taken a small section of those Authors to show you their Fame Name, so it gives you some ideas.

All of the people you see above are Coaches, Trainers, Mentors and/or Consultants, so it is easy for them to get swept up in an already flooded industry.

They were drowning in the sea of *sameness*.

So the first thing I did was take them through the 7-Step Brand Kickstarter to create their brand positioning strategy and get their Fame Name in place. As you can see, they each now have a Fame Name that positions their brand to exactly match what their ideal customers want. As a result of this branding process, they are now highly in demand, charging what they are worth and busier than they've ever been.

So, let's now work on your Fame Name.

Step One...

List some important keywords you want to be known for.

Trish Carr of The Women's Prosperity Network is paid thousands of dollars per day to train companies how to sell more. She shows them how to turn their mouth into money and has built her reputation as *The Results Revolutionary*. Some of the keywords that Trish used whilst creating her Fame Name would have been Money, Sales, Sell More, Turn Your Mouth Into Money, Results, etc. These were just a few of the keywords she came up with to start her Fame Name process.

Now it's your turn. What do you want to be most known and remembered for? Start by listing below at least five to ten keywords that you most want to be known for...

____

____

____

Step Two...

Now list some important keywords around the results you deliver. For example, Gosia Gorna has a successful business supporting her clients to release their fears. *Release* is what she does as she doesn't just relieve her clients fear, she releases it, so it is gone forever.

Her Fame Name *The Fear Releaser* is perfect because FEAR is what she is building her name in; and Releaser is what she does.

Now it's your turn.

What results do you consistently leave your clients with?

Again, list five to ten different options...

____

____

____

Step Three...

Now let's bring it all together and play with picking different words from your answers in both step one and two, bringing them together to play with different variations of Your Fame Name...

____

____

____

Congratulations! Now you need to test it! The best way to test it is to reach out to some people you already know that you'd love to work with and ask them which is their favourite out of your top three choices. You can also post your choices on social media to create extra publicity, but the only people whose opinion really matters are those that are going to spend money with you!

Remember to watch the additional training I created to help make this process even easier for you.

Here's the link: *bit.ly/pivotgrowbrand* and I shall look forward to hearing what you come up with!

See you on the other side

Lots of love, Sammy xx

About Sammy Blindell

Sammy is a multi-award-winning international speaker, 8 times best-selling author, CEO of Brand Builders Club and Founder of One Drop Movement.

Having spent thirteen years in branding before launching her first business in 2002, Sammy built six more companies in the business growth sector. She launched her online branding resource in 2014, taking it from £0 to £18,000 of monthly revenue in twelve weeks with her first book and online program, building significant wealth before turning forty.

In February 2017 she launched Brand Builders Club, which has hundreds of members Internationally. Finally, her Global movement *www.OneDropMovement.com* was founded in April 2019 to celebrate the ripple that is created when Changemakers collaborate rather than compete.

Sammy has created 72 online products and 1000+ online courses to show others how to accomplish in just a few months what it takes most business owners a lifetime to achieve.

Now it's your turn!

Contact Sammy Blindell

Website: *www.SammyBlindell.com*

Email: *sammy@howtobuildabrand.org*

Join Sammy in The Brand Builders Club:
https://lite.brandbuilders.club/member

Follow me on:

Facebook: *https://www.facebook.com/SammyBlindellOfficial*

Twitter: *https://twitter.com/SammyBlindell*

LinkedIn: *https://www.linkedin.com/in/sammyblindellthebrandbuilder*

Instagram: *https://www.instagram.com/sammyblindell*

Business Rejuvenation In Uncertain Times

Matthew Newnham

"Give me a lever long enough and a fulcrum on which to place it, and I shall move the world." - Archimedes

Many business owners are feeling uncertainty, pressure, doubts and fears in the current environment. You may feel that way. In response, you may be considering a change in direction for your business. Or you may be thinking it's best to maintain your current course.

Either way, I'd like to share what I have found to be the most direct, lowest-risk approach to positioning and growing your business safely and sustainably in any economic climate.

This is based on my work with clients around the world over the past decade to rejuvenate their positioning, their message and their business. I'm laying out as much as I can of my Soul Centred Branding process here so you can start enjoying those benefits.

Onwards...

Rising Above Everyone Else

February 2020, Glasgow. 20-year-old Swedish pole vaulter Armondo Duplantis does what most experts thought might never happen. He breaks the 27-year-old world record set by Sergey Bubka, the greatest pole vaulter ever, with more titles than any other athlete in history.

To do this, Duplantis has to sprint down the runway at over 22mph, plant his pole, pivot 180 degrees and launch himself over a bar 6.18 metres overhead, 3.5 times his own height. But talent, skill and dedication is only half of the story behind his growing global profile.

Competitive athletics has all but been shut down in 2020. The Tokyo Olympics have been postponed and all public competitions have been cancelled except a few socially distanced events. Even so, 'Mondo' has managed to inject fresh excitement into athletics this year.

Spectators love his athletic feats and his passion. He relates to them and they reciprocate.

As a result, he has rapidly become a major star on the world athletics stage.

The Mondo Approach To Engaging Brand-Building

Professional sport is not just competition between athletes; it's also an entertainment product. In the entertainment world, it takes expertise, excellence and emotional connection to build a winning business.

World-class vaulting plus emotional connection has enabled Mondo to build an enthusiastic following of raving fans. There are other phenomenal sportspeople who are at the top of their game but cannot connect nearly as well. The same is true for businesses - and it shows.

What Emotion Can Do For Your Business

Most business owners agree intellectually the old adage that people buy on emotion then justify their decision with logic. However, few business owners seem to believe it's true for them and their business, because they rarely seem to act on it. That's costly if understandable.

For starters, we want to be seen as serious, credible people. So it's natural to prefer your customers to buy from you based on your excellent quality and *logical* advantages over the alternatives, ahead of any good feelings they may have about you.

Then there's the fear of being salesy and manipulative. So much marketing and sales is a turn-off, because it feels pushy or manipulative or fails to connect. But what if our best clients actually also want positive emotional outcomes in addition to the results we deliver?

We know we buy to solve problems. As long as we have the problem, we endure unwanted emotions like frustration or fear. When the problem is solved, we experience relief and other pleasant emotions. And yet, few businesses use this insight much, if at all.

Of course, it's vital to note that we're talking about the appropriate type and level of emotions for you, your ideal audience and your business. Now let's put this concept to work.

The 40/40/20 Rule For Winning More Business

Legendary direct response marketer Ed Meyer was one of the original *Ad Men* in New York. He started and ran one of the most successful ad agencies in the world for 50 years before selling his firm to global giant WPP and retiring.

Meyer was credited with being the first to systematically measure which campaigns increased sales versus the ones that underperformed or failed. Over his five decades of spending hundreds of millions of dollars on ads, Meyer's analysis led to his 40/40/20 Rule:

- 40% of all successful marketing campaigns win based on how good the offer is.
- Another 40% of success comes from how receptive the audience is to the offer.
- The final 20% comes from how well the sales copy and graphics perform.

So we can maximise 80% of our sales by offering what people really want to those who want it the most, without having to hope our marketing wins the sale. Therefore, that's where we should focus most of our efforts. How do we go about that?

"Where Are You An Animal?"

I was on a webinar years ago where the presenter put up a slide asking, *Where are you an animal?* He wanted us to nail down where we're at our best and deliver the most value to our clients. This is vital if you want your business to be recognised as having distinctive value.

But for various reasons, most people aren't aware of their *superpower*. Plus, they struggle to find it on their own. Even worse, there is a strong tendency to play it too safe, reverting to the skills and experience you'd list if you were applying for a job. Those are rarely on the money.

Instead, you want to zero in on the essence of what you do for others that comes most naturally and provides the biggest positive outcomes for those you're helping. To be clear, we're focused on what's genuinely tangible and valuable, with no boasting or hype.

I've been helping business owners do this since 2010, and my clients are pleasantly surprised by the findings. This exercise reveals much stronger positioning that resonates with them, strengthens their perceived value significantly and breathes new life into their business.

A highly accomplished entrepreneur friend of mine said: "It's like having a conversation with myself, except I couldn't have had that conversation on my own." (Others say the same.)

For a free resource to help you discover your superpower(s) for yourself please see my bio below. This resource is based on over 50,000 private consults globally over 38 years and people love it. (I've also used it with all my Soul Centred Branding clients since 2010.)

Which Problems Do You Care About Solving?

Once you've identified your superpower, we need to put it to work delivering value. To do that you need to identify the highest value problem you can solve and all the positive benefits you deliver as a result - both on a practical level and the resulting emotional outcomes.

Then ask yourself: Why do you care about delivering these outcomes? It doesn't have to be some big public statement (we all have our reasons and handle them differently). But you're far more likely to deliver on those emotional outcomes if you genuinely care.

Important: Your results can be solid and transactional, or you can also help deliver your clients' desired emotional outcomes. Then your service is transformational. You choose.

For example, one of our clients is an accountant who cares deeply about financial health and the peace of mind it brings. She provides high-end bookkeeping for businesses and high net worth individuals across the US and in Europe. Her clients come to her when they have money leaks and worries that aren't getting dealt with by their other professional advisors.

She identifies the leaks, typically within minutes, then sets up systems and processes to stop the leaks from recurring. Her clients are better off financially and they are no longer haunted by money worries. Their relief is immense, tangible and ongoing. Her clients are delighted.

We call her service *Fast-Acting Financial Relief* (picture two *plop-plop, fizz-fizz* tablets). And her transformational benefits set her apart from the countless other bookkeeping firms.

Your What Informs Your Who

It's great to think of your customers first. I've lost track of how many business owners fall in love with their own idea so deeply that they can't see beyond themselves to their customers.

However, it's also almost impossible to focus properly on your customers until you're really clear about your superpower and how you can use it to help others. (I've seen too many get stuck on this, sometimes with tragic consequences.)

In practice, there is usually a back-and-forth art to triangulating between your *What* and your *Who*. It requires figuring out the specific problems they have that you're going to help solve, including being clear on what their emotional state will be before and after you help them.

How Much Do You Care? Show Them

It's also highly advisable that you genuinely care about your chosen audience, as well as the problems you've chosen to help solve. That care (and passion, if that's how you roll) will be read by your audience and customers in all kinds of ways. If you have it, put it to use.

Another client of ours is an IP lawyer in the US whose clients typically come to her when they're being threatened with legal proceedings. These clients are very worried about how much the legal action could cost them, financially and in terms of their intellectual property.

Our client is exceptionally skilled at quickly de-escalating and defusing lawsuits, resolving them far more quickly and affordably than other lawyers. She always starts with getting clear on what her clients truly desire for their outcomes, in business and in life. She listens closely.

Through her focus and expertise, she's able to reassure her clients quickly, addressing their doubts and fears directly and transparently. That's uncommon. But she goes further: she treats her clients like family. That's why they love her, sing her praises and stick with her for years.

She transforms a stressful purchase of a transactional service to a happy transformational one.

So, What Is It You Do Exactly?

For many business owners, this is one of the toughest questions they face. They struggle to answer with confidence, in a natural way that reflects and inspires them.

My hope is that the concepts in this chapter will help you just that, so that you can have more of the business that you really want, and therefore live the life you desire. As I say to my clients, I regard this as sacred work. After all, our life and opportunities are so precious.

"Understand that the right to choose your own path is a sacred privilege. Use it. Dwell in possibility." - Oprah Winfrey

If you would like to have a virtual coffee to look at where you're at with your strategic positioning or messaging, feel free to get in touch with me via the links below.

About Matthew Newnham

Matthew Newnham is a brand positioning specialist who helps business owners clarify and communicate their value, to become respected thought leaders and grow their business more naturally with less effort.

Along with his great friend Nicholas Haines, Matthew is co-founder at Five Institute, home of The Vitality Test, which Nick created, based on 50,000 private consultations over 38 years.

20,000 people have taken it globally and people say it's the most insightful personality test they've ever experienced.

Discover your superpower and how it can transform your business. Take the free online Vitality Test here *https://www.fiveinstitute.com* then contact Matthew for a free personalised walkthrough of your results.

Contact Matthew Newnham

RepositionMe Brand Positioning services:
https://repositionme.com/

LinkedIn at: *https://www.linkedin.com/in/matthewnewnham*

LinkedIn-based Thought Leadership services:
https://www.linkedsure.com

Email: *matthew@repositionme.com*

All Companies Can Pivot And Grow With Data

Mike Bugembe

Information is power, and every company, regardless of size or industry, can experience the transformational growth that the world of data promises.

The prevailing public opinion that data is only for large corporations or innovative start-ups from Silicon Valley is far from the truth. In fact, it would be reasonable to argue that any business (post the 2020 pandemic) cannot survive or thrive without understanding how they can pivot and grow with data.

Customers are now digital-first, and the internet has become the most effective way for businesses to continue trading. Any business with a website, a social media presence, or one that accepts electronic payments will collect data about customer habits, demographics, and so much more. This data is packed with tremendous growth potential, enabling all businesses to gain access to transformational insights, make impactful decisions, and grow.

Simply put, when data is analysed and translated into information, it can help all businesses become smarter, more productive, and more efficient. When used correctly, data will create a noticeable competitive advantage and simultaneously boost conversions, profits, and revenue.

Data will supercharge your ability to pivot and grow.

What Can You Do With Data?

There is almost an infinite number of uses for data, including but not limited to the ability to:

- More effectively market to customers
- Design products that meet specific customer needs
- Identify growth opportunities
- Reveal new sources of revenue
- Forecast more accurately

Sadly, we often overcomplicate our understanding of where data will add transformational value to an organisation. I usually have to stress this point when working with senior executives. If there is only one thing that you take away, it is this - Data has only one major use case, supporting effective decision-making.

Amazons complex recommendation engine helps Amazon decide what additional products to serve to the customer in order to maximise basket size. The speedometer in your car provides data that enables you to decide whether to press the brake or the accelerator.

This may seem obvious, as we often come across the term "data for decision making" in articles, blogs, and product launches. However, my challenge is that if "data for decision-making" is obvious, then surely, organisations should all know all the key decisions that impact growth? Sadly, when many are asked this question, they flounder.

Understanding the key decisions that affect your core growth metrics is a non-negotiable requirement to see value from data.

Broadly speaking, to effectively pivot and grow, business owners, managers, and executives have to make crucial decisions to

- Acquire more customers
- Optimise the value from customers
- Increase retention

There are many factors to consider when making decisions in these critical areas, and your choices are to either rely on gut instinct or combine your experience with new and actionable insights made available with data. Smart individuals choose to work with data. Others are merely guessing, which often means their results are either lucky or wrong.

The proof, however, is in the numbers. I have personally worked with companies that have grown fivefold by using Twitter and Facebook data to better understand what makes their customers tick. Others have grown their total number of customers by addressing one small aspect of their product that isn't visible to the human eye but obvious when looking at the data.

I have done some work with companies that have seen more than 65% growth in customer retention by analysing their own internal customer behavioural data. There are well-documented case studies of even street vendors finding over 30% growth hidden in their customers' geographic data. These benefits are not restricted to commercial endeavours. Data has also been transformational in crime reduction, increased generosity in the charity space, early detection of mental health issues in the medical space, and so much more. There are no limits to the growth potential that data promises.

Despite all the excitement and potential, very few organisations have realised these benefits. Fear, misinformation, and a lack of understanding are key obstacles that prevent organisations from even starting their journey with data.

This chapter will guide you through three essential best practices that will place you firmly on the path to realising value from data.

1. Become Data Literate

Understanding how to work with data has typically been a technical task, but this is one of the industry's biggest misconceptions. There is a clear correlation between data literate business users and the effectiveness of their business decisions. Rather than leave the interpretation entirely in a technical analyst's hands, a business user adds a dimension that generates transformative value to the data.

In a world increasingly powered by data, an organisation's ability to pivot and grow will be heavily dependent on all of its non-technical employees and executives abilities to append data to their experience, intuition and ability to strategize.

Data can answer a myriad of questions that your company is asking, but to truly see value from data, you must address the questions that will make a meaningful difference to your company's goals and objectives. To do this, you need to know the business well and who knows the business better than the business users and leaders.

Value from data comes when it is intentionally goal-focused, and no one understands the company's goals better than its executives and top leadership. They have the bird's eye view and insight to steer data in the direction that it should go while avoiding the time and money consuming rabbit holes that one could easily fall into.

Today in what some would call a data-driven economy, understanding how to work with data is as important as reading, writing, and typing. As we move into an increasingly machine-driven business environment, where data drives business growth, every role will require the skills to read, work with, and create compelling business cases with data.

The cold facts are that data has the power to change your businesses, but only when it can be seen and understood correctly. To do that, you will need to be data literate.

Data literacy is the ability to read, work with, analyse and communicate with data. It's a skill that empowers every employee to ask the right questions, build knowledge, make decisions, and communicate meaning to others.

Fortunately, today, there are many non-technical courses available to help business executives build their data capabilities and extract valuable insights, which will enable them to lead with data-informed decisions to pivot and grow their business.

The idea that you need to have a technical background to generate real insight from data is entirely false; everyone can see and understand data. It is not as complicated as it sounds. Once you have passed the quick learning curve, data wrangling will become very profitable.

2. Collect The Right Data

We live in a world where data is literally everywhere. The challenge is collecting the right data for the right purpose. If you get this step wrong, it will be almost impossible to generate any meaningful value from data. Bad data leads to bad decisions.

Your objective is to collect meaningful data. That means data that leads to actionable insight and informs business decisions. More often than not, businesses choose metrics that look good but do not help make the right decisions to grow - these are called vanity metrics.

While they look great on paper, the gloss on vanity metrics quickly fades when you try and use them to explain essential business outcomes like ROI or customer lifetime value. A common vanity metric that I have come across is data on traffic sources to a website. I met a business owner who boasted about how much traffic they have from Facebook and decided to continue to invest heavily in growing traffic from that source. When you looked deeper at the right metrics, it was clear that there was no ROI from Facebook. It was losing them money. The right metrics showed that while other sources couldn't demonstrate the same traffic magnitude, they could demonstrate the greater revenue-generating value. Investment in the more valuable sources would have resulted in immediate double-digit growth.

There are three key steps that you should follow to avoid collecting poor data, but you must start with the key company goals and decisions. Data must always be goal focussed. Earlier in this chapter, we highlighted several key decisions that most companies will make to pivot and grow. These included finding new customers, increasing retention and so on.

To understand what data to capture:

1. Consider which of those goals is most problematic or has the largest upside potential.

2. Identify the relevant pain points in the chosen goal. Consider the problems, challenges and key questions that the data needs to solve.

3. Triangulate by adding additional points of data. Each data set you acquire provides you with a unique point of view of your business operations and external environment. While insightful on their own, a single data set rarely provides the complete picture. Similar to vanity metrics, single data sets typically only show half the story. Consider aggregating data from different sources, allowing you to have multiple points-of-view and provide a more holistic perspective.

When a business can identify, track, and improve the right metrics, they get a clear picture of when they add value to their business and when they are not. Thus, it is important to take the time necessary to think about the data that you are collecting.

3. Extract The Story From Data

Data is just a collection of numbers until you turn it into a story. No matter how advanced your infrastructure is, it will not provide you with any insights until you interrogate it and ask the right questions. The approach of merely pulling together tables of numbers and graphs can be overwhelming without adding a narrative to the data. Narrative is uniquely human, while data is definitively inhuman, rigid, and lifeless. How we reconcile these two is the key to recognising value from data.

Any great narrative from data explains what happened, why it is important, what is likely to happen, and suggestions on how you can make the insight more actionable. Yet this can still be difficult to extract from tables of data.

One approach to pulling out a great narrative is to look at trends. A trend quantifies and explains data patterns over time. It shows the data at certain points in the past and any follow-on movements, either upward or downwards. Data represented in this way can also help you understand how the demand for your products or services will change over time and what will prompt that change. You can track trends in whatever time frame works best for your business, day-by-day, week-by-week, monthly or quarterly.

Trends will allow you to spot and monitor behaviours and patterns that will help you understand what happened, why it happened, and which direction things are likely to be headed. Until recently, trend analysis and prediction often came down to 'gut instinct'. Now, data is taking a lot of the guesswork out of that process.

There is a lot of information in this article, and with my excitement and enthusiasm for what I have seen data do, I could write a lot more. The key points to remember are that data will help you pivot and grow.

All you have to do is take some time to learn a bit more about it, collect the right data, and tell the data story. Crack those three steps, and you will genuinely see the transformational value that data will add to your organisation.

"When you have mastered numbers, you will in fact no longer be reading numbers, any more than you read words when reading books. You will be reading meanings."

William Edward Burghardt Du Bois

About Mike Bugembe

Mike is a bestselling author, international speaker, and executive adviser in data and AI. He runs an AI training and consulting company called LENS.AI, which helps business owners and executives learn essential data skills. Before that, he was the chief analytics officer at *JustGiving.com* where his team transformed the world of giving by using algorithms to raise millions for charity. He has won several awards and is regarded as one of the most influential people in the world on data.

Working with product leaders from organisations like Facebook, Netflix, Amazon and Spotify, Mike published his unique approach to generating value from data in his best-selling book *Cracking the Data Code*. It is used as a blueprint on data for many large businesses. He is now a sought-after consultant advising start-ups and large established companies on creating and generating value from investments in the world of data and AI.

Relevant links

https://www.forbes.com/sites/tommywilliams1/2019/02/28/meet-mike-bugembe-the-data-scientist-who-helped-people-give-more-to-charity/#5b180b557de2

www.lens.ai

www.mikebugembe.com

https://uk.linkedin.com/in/mikebugembe

Unlocking Collective Intelligence To Drive Positive Change

Marissa Ellis

The number one, often overlooked, goal in business is to remain relevant.

Relevance is what drives sales, great customer experiences, value creation and profit. Your products and services must be relevant to your customers. Your solutions must help them solve pressing and painful problems. Without relevance your business will lose market share, customer loyalty and revenue; and it will ultimately fail.

Figure 1 Relevance

Kodak lost relevance. They monopolised over 85% of the film and camera market in 1976 and filed for bankruptcy in 2012. They did not keep up with, never mind lead, the digital revolution. Blind optimism and riding on the coat-tails of previous success does not bring long term success.

"The goal of a startup is to figure out the right thing to build – the thing that customers want to pay money for – as quickly as possible."

Eric Ries, *The Lean Startup* [1]

Eric Ries inspired entrepreneurs globally with his adaptation of Toyota's lean manufacturing principles for the start-up world. People started to navigate the Build-Measure-Learn loop as they experimented rapidly to find the business model that worked for them. New waves of intrapreneurs were created within large corporates who also recognised that innovation was not just something for the start-ups. Innovation is the key to remaining relevant.

Business is a journey and not a destination. Once a business finds relevance their job is not done; their ongoing mission is to remain relevant. Pivoting and growth are tactics to remain relevant. Growth is about scale – doing more, earning more, growing market share, building your brand, etc. Pivoting is about focus and direction. Growth is pushing down on the accelerator and pivoting is controlling the steering wheel of your business.

Businesses must change constantly in order to:

- Drive innovation and continuous improvement.

- Build resilience in order to respond rapidly to circumstances outside their control.
- Continually ensure their goals are the ones that will deliver most impact.
- Truly serve the evolving and diverse needs of their customers.

The only real constant in business is change. Businesses that recognise that change is constant are more able to embrace it, navigate it successfully and remain relevant. This means building an operating rhythm into your business that enables constant change – and if business is all about change, what is your job as a business leader?

Imagine for a moment if all business leaders around the world set themselves this single goal:

'To unlock collective intelligence to drive positive change'.

Think about how transformational this could be. Shifting your mindset to examine your role in this new way will not only help you achieve greater business success, it will make the world a better place.

There are several elements to this aspirational goal. Firstly, it is about recognising the power of diversity and inclusion and understanding that no one of us is greater than us all. Secondly, it is about change, so we need to equip ourselves with the tools to navigate change successfully and continuously. Lastly, but not least, it is about recognising that business is not all about profit. Businesses have a profound impact on the world and leaders have a responsibility to ensure this impact is a positive one.

ING is a bank. Their purpose is not to make as much money as possible. Their purpose is empowering people to stay a step ahead in life and in business. This purpose guides them in everything they do.

"Purpose is one of the top motivators on the planet."

Daniel H. Pink, Drive [2]

People – and therefore businesses – are connected to a deeper purpose: a desire to leave the world in a better place than they found it. Meaningful work is the cornerstone of motivation.

A factory worker was interviewed during the Coronavirus pandemic. His factory had halted all normal production and they were now working around the clock to make precision parts for ventilators. He said that they have never worked so hard, yet they are happy to be making a difference. Their working environment has actually improved, as everyone knows what they are doing is saving lives.

A critical prerequisite for human excellence is purpose. This instils a deep belief that both people and situations can change for the better.

People who are working towards something that is bigger than themselves are some of the most highly motivated and productive people in the world.

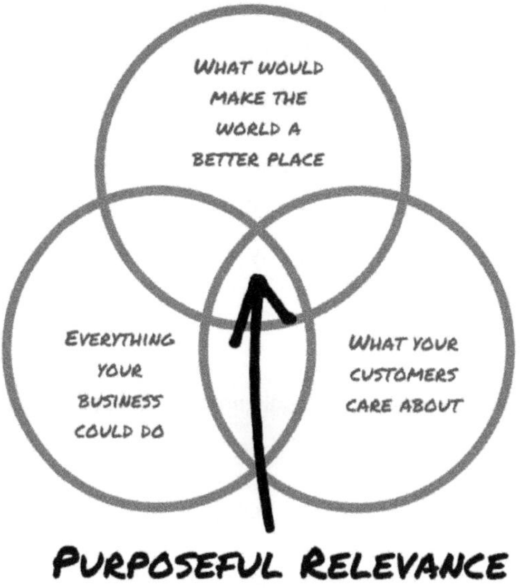

Figure 2 Purposeful Relevance

How can leaders that choose to embark upon this continuous journey of purposeful relevance be successful?

The villain in our story is the status quo. The status quo tells us that what we have always done is best. The status quo stops us from asking 'why' and from challenging ourselves to do better. The status quo is blighted by centuries of perpetual bias, discrimination and inequality. The status quo blocks progress: The World Economic Forum predicts that it will take 99.5 years to close the gender gap.[3]

Humans have a natural bias for the status quo. This is an emotional connection to the current state, irrespective of the merits of the current state or alternative options. We all have many biases that need to be countered to drive inclusive change. Affinity bias makes us more amenable to people like us. Groupthink steers our opinions to align with others. Stereotyping encourages us to make (often incorrect) assumptions about others. Confirmation bias makes us listen only to information that confirms our preconceptions.

As well as countering bias, the brave leaders who rise to the challenge of unlocking collective intelligence to drive positive change will face many other challenges along the way, such as:

- Lack of clarity, consistency or alignment on direction, strategy or vision.
- Lack of buy in, engagement or inclusion.
- Lack of diverse thinking where loudest voices dominate.
- Talk not being translated into action.
- Lack of transparency, visibility or common understanding across teams and people.
- Lack of agility in working practices.
- Too much information and complexity.

To challenge the status quo, we need redefine what success looks like.

There is growing and widely accepted research to show that diversity and inclusion is good for business.[4] Whatever your aspirations, you should always consider the impact to everyone, not only the majority groups. Diversity and inclusion should be built into the core of every business, not just because it is the right thing to do, but because it:

- Drives higher performance and increased financial returns.

- Reduces risk and increases competitive advantage.
- Improves customer experience and inspires better solutions.
- Enhances wellbeing, creates equality and positive social impact.
- Inspires innovation and enables complex change.

What is also clear is that the pace of change in business has never been so rapid. Organisations that do not continue to innovate are at risk of getting left behind. As innovation practices mature and become a fundamental part of business, it is critical that diversity and inclusion sits at the heart of these practices. When companies establish inclusive business cultures and policies, they are more likely to report an increase in creativity, innovation, openness and better assessment of customer interest and demand.[4]

Business practices that lack 'inclusive thinking' create huge blind spots that make relevance all that harder to achieve. There can also be unintended consequences, such as propagation of discrimination in decision making engines, or products that only serve limited audiences.

There is no shortage of real-life examples: the voice-recognition system that only recognised male voices, the face-recognition technology that tagged black people as gorillas and the automated soap dispenser that only worked with white hands.

Inclusive innovation is about catering for everyone. This means:

- Creating an authentic portrait of your customers, serving everyone in your target market equally well.

- Diverse, inclusive and representative participation in the innovation process to leverage cognitive diversity and gain broader perspectives.
- Countering bias, echo chambers and blind spots.
- Catering for diverse needs and avoiding unintentional exclusion.
- Serving underrepresented, underserved or marginalised groups or markets.
- Creating a sense of belonging across difference in a world of hyper-personalised customer experience.
- Systematically considering the impact, ethical and environmental implications and unintended consequences of innovation and not just focusing on the bottom line.

The heroes in our story are the changemakers who find their purpose and embark on a mission to make a difference in the world. A profound shift in thinking is required to defeat our villain, the status quo.

The Change Canvas was created to serve our heroes and to accelerate the pace of change. It is a simple, iterative framework that covers three important elements of change:

- **Reflection** – looking back to understand where we are now, the problems we are trying to solve and why change is needed.
- **Vision** – looking forward to define what success looks like and set goals for success.
- **Progress** – generating ideas, taking action and celebrating results.

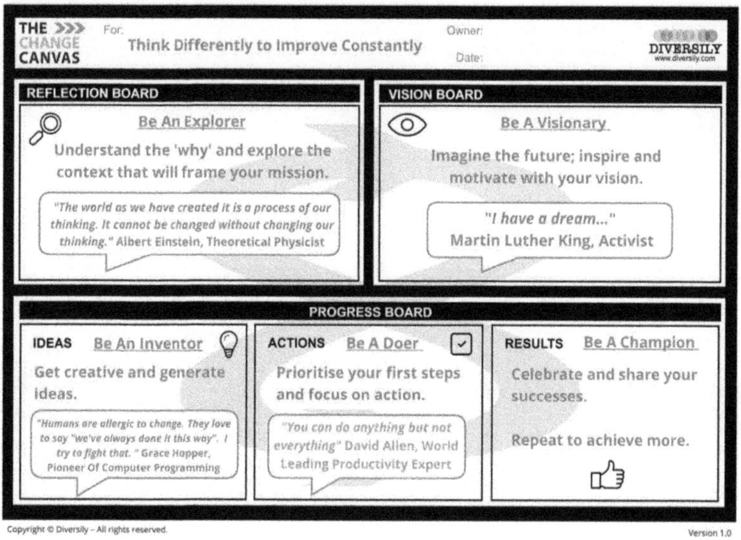

Figure 3 The Change Canvas

The Change Canvas is not just a visual framework, it is a methodology for making positive and inclusive change happen. Organisations of all types and sizes around the world are using it to unite and to drive forward their collective mission. The approach is centred on core principles of inclusion, collaboration and agility with a strong bias towards action.

If growth is putting your foot on the accelerator and pivoting is your steering wheel, then The Change Canvas is your map. It is your single source of truth that guides you on your path, uniting everyone to contribute to your mission.

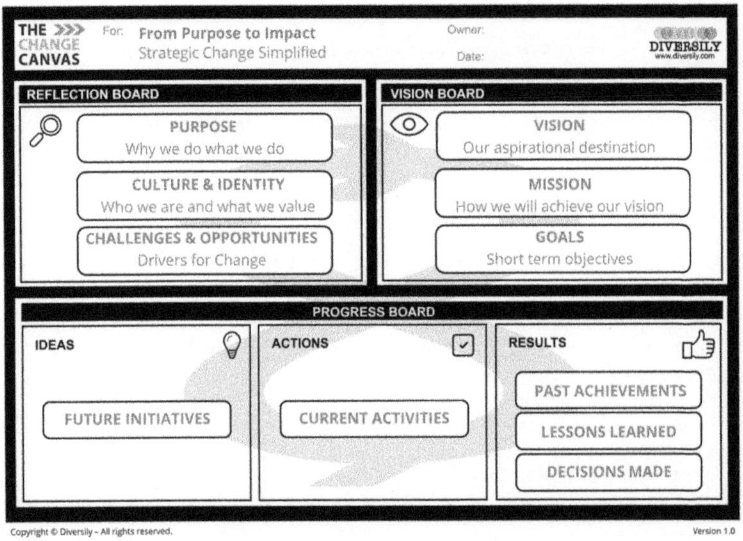

Figure 4 The Building Blocks of Change

Distilling your business down to these key elements, shown in The Change Canvas above, is incredibly powerful as it forces important conversations and helps you focus on what matters.

The Change Canvas methodology provides a proven, systematic approach for a continuous Debate-Decide-Do cycle. This powers growth and continuous course correction and encourages teams to build five key levers for success into their operating rhythm.

- A sense of purpose and a culture of belonging.
- Clarity of long-term vision and short-term focus.
- Diversity of ideas.
- Empowered, proactive individuals.
- Agility and celebration of success.

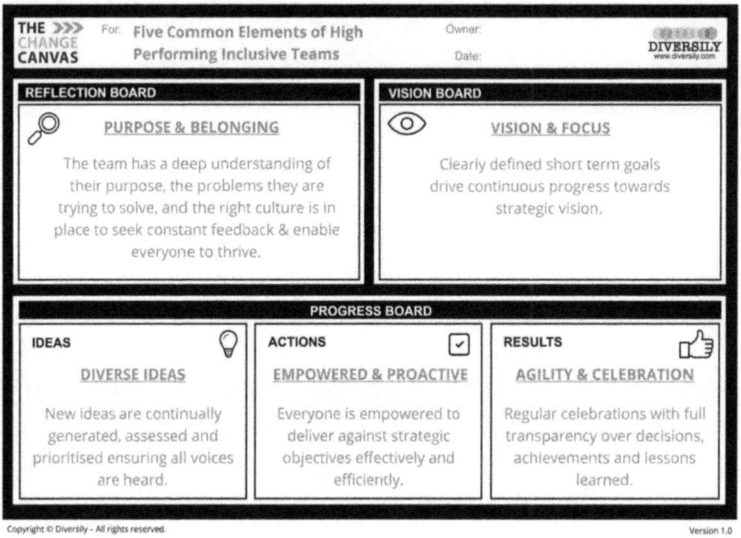

Figure 5 Five Levers for High Performing Inclusive Teams

Challenging yourself in these areas can help you unlock potential areas for improvement within your team.

The Change Canvas is gaining traction fast around the world. Organisations of all types and sizes are using it as a framework for driving strategic change inclusively.[5]

- A global consulting team use it for strategic planning and to drive everything they do.
- A not-for-profit organisation use it to unite and align over 70 volunteers to deliver their mission on a part-time, remote, asynchronous basis.
- A global Fintech use it to manage transformation programmes and drive collaboration across the business.
- A global bank used it to help them drive culturally inclusive innovation.

The philosophy is one of creating teams that are D.E.F.T.

- Directional
- Empowering
- Focused
- Transparent

Learning to think inclusively will profoundly change the way you see the world. It will remove blind spots, open your eyes to new possibilities and change the decisions you make. Once you start doing it, it is very difficult to go back. It is something that becomes intrinsically part of everything you do. Inclusive leadership unlocks collective intelligence and delivers richer outcomes. It also opens access to the best talent globally and maximises market reach.

Your number one goal in business is to remain relevant. Connecting to a deeper purpose will guide your mission through pivots and growth. Diversity and inclusion are not side-line considerations – they are fundamental levers for business success. Your job as a leader is to unlock collective intelligence to drive positive change. The Change Canvas was created to empower heroes like you.

References

1. Reis, E. (2011). The Lean Startup: How Today's Entrepreneurs Use Continuous Innovation to Create Radically Successful Businesses

2. Pink, D. (2011). Drive: The Surprising Truth About What Motivates Us

3. World Economic Forum (2020), Global Gender Gap Report 2020

4. Catalyst (2020). Quick Take: Why Diversity and Inclusion Matter

5. For more information visit www.diversily.com

About Marissa Ellis

Marissa Ellis is an advisor, strategist and speaker. She is the founder of *www.diversily.com* and the creator of The Change Canvas and other business frameworks that are used around the world to drive positive change.

Marissa helps business leaders, changemakers and entrepreneurs deliver impactful and inclusive strategic change. She helps organisations take advantage of the Diversily Toolkit to build high performing inclusive teams, create more inclusive experiences, launch new products and services, drive business transformation and develop leaders.

Marissa is a passionate advocate for equality, diversity and inclusion and her personal mission is to help more people to 'think inclusively'.

She has over 20 years of experience in the tech sector, from well-known names such as Reuters, Barclays and lastminute.com, to high growth start-ups and accelerators. She has deep expertise in digital innovation, Fintech, inclusion, leadership and change.

Marissa holds a first-class honours MSci Masters degree in Mathematics.

Contact Marissa Ellis

www.diversily.com

Twitter: *@diversily*

LinkedIn: *https://www.linkedin.com/in/marissaellis*

LinkedIn Diversily: *https://www.linkedin.com/company/diversily*

The Sales Paradox

Baiju Solanki

Introduction

Sales can be a dirty word for a lot of people: the perception of sleazy, pushy tactics and manipulative behaviours. However, we are living in a world now where we are dealing with a very sophisticated market, they know what they want, they know where to look and they are in control of when, where and who they want to buy it from.

Google did a study in 2011 on how customers behave online around buying habits called Zero Moment of Truth (ZMOT).

Google defines ZMOT simply as a shared truth (somebody's subjective experience) that influences a purchase decision.

With this level of sophistication that the market has, it is imperative to get your house in order. Here is where I talk about the three areas you need to focus on.

There are three areas around sales that you need to look at when you think about selling:

- Your Mindset - Your Inner Game
- Your Strategy - Your Game Plan
- Your Actions - Your Outer Game

Your Mindset - Your Inner Game

The perception is that sales is about strategy and what action you take, which it is, as we will address, but the foundation is your mindset. I want to reframe what sales is from the start, as most of what will be talked about here will be about serving the customer.

- Sales is serving.

- Sales is serving.
- Sales is serving.

This is so true now, it has always been true and it is even truer in the world we currently live in.

Whether you are selling a product, service or both, you have a duty to serve your customer so they get value.

Now, why is selling so important? Without sales, there is no money; no money means there is no business.

Why am I calling this the sales paradox? Because I want to shift your thinking from you selling, to you creating an environment where your customers can happily and willingly buy from you.

The principals of sales will always be the same; except we now have many more resources.

What is key is the sales process and the environment that you create for the buying experience to occur. Think Amazon.

Why Sales Never Changes And Is Always Different

So what is the paradox? Sales is not about you. Yes, you need to generate money for your business. This is just the consequence of your activity.

Your activity is about the process. The paradox is that it is about the customer. The customer wants to buy stuff. They want to be able to spend their money. Your duty is to make it easy for them to buy.

So, why do people buy?

- To solve a problem
- To get a shortcut
- To be protected
- To enjoy their life
- To provide convenience
- To make their life easier

Whatever you are selling, from this moment onwards, make it ONLY about serving. With this shift in mindset, you now have no more excuses to not shout about your products and services.

Your Strategy - Your Game Plan

Your sales strategy needs to focus on three areas

- Digital
- Visibility
- Authority

Digital

There is no excuse not to use the many free or low-cost digital resources to either create a sales environment or make it seamless for the customer to buy from you, as demonstrated by the Zero Moment of Truth Study mentioned earlier.

Now here, we are not talking about creating your own

mini Amazon, but just be aware of what digital resources are available to make your customer experience and your business operations more efficient.

Ignorance is not an excuse. It's not a choice.

There was a time when if you ran a business, depending on what you were selling, you either had an office, factory or shop.

Now it's not just about a website, it's about the ways you can use integrators, APIs, webinars, social media platforms and payment gateways.

Whatever your business and whatever you are selling there is a digital resource or solution to it. There are too many to mention them here. The key is to map out what you want your customer experience to be and what the sales process will be, then reach out to people who are in the digital space and research what is out there.

You will be surprised what you will find. If you don't know where to start, reach out to me and I'll show you where to start depending on what your business is.

Visibility

The second strategy you need to maximise is visibility. Again, no excuses here. Never before and especially in the times we live in, has visibility been so important. And relatively easy.

With visibility you have eyeballs. Sounds simple, doesn't it? You'd be surprised how many businesses don't maximise or even utilise all the ways to be visible.

This is where your mindset is key. You have to think outside the box here. Think about how you make it easy for your customer to find you. People are spending so much time online, mainly for entertainment. Are you thinking about how to intercept their experience with your product and services?

When you are aware of the numerous digital resources available, you will start to discover the many ways you can be more visible to your market.

One key aspect of visibility is how you look and seem attractive. You have to be a magnet. When a magnet gets to a critical distance with a metal object it pulls it in. That's exactly how it works with visibility. All you need to do is get enough customers close enough to your product and services before they will be compelled to take action without you having to do anything.

A lot of the sale is done when you don't even know it. People are looking at stuff, without acknowledging with likes or comments. They are making decisions out of your sight.

Explore all the ways your products and services can be visible to ensure the sale is one where the buyer buys and you don't need to sell.

Authority

People buy from people who they trust and display authority. When you have authority either for your product or service or the market you are in, the conversation with the customer becomes easier.

The barrier or potential resistance the customer may have,

disappears because there is intrinsic trust coming from a place of authority.

So how can this be done? Ask yourself what would you want to see, feel and understand about your product or service that would make someone feel you have authority in your market segment?

Your Actions - Your Outer Game

Without actions, nothing happens. This is the third game you have to conquer. Actually what you have to conquer is how consistent you are in your actions.

The best sales technique around actions is conversation. The more conversations you have, the more opportunities you have to generate sales.

Now looking back on the different strategies, especially digital, the conversation isn't just 121 face-to-face conversations; it's conversations that take place online, on social media, forums and groups.

When you have conversations you create opportunities too, because the chance of new ideas can be discussed. However, it is very easy to just let these conversations run and run.

This is where your mindset is key. Don't be afraid to make sure the audience is aware of what is available and how they can experience your product or service. In marketing language this is called a call to action.

A more empowered approach is creating a buying environment.

In conclusion, sales will never change, what will change are the resources available. These resources will make the experience of your market more customer-centric and your model much more effective. A business should always be pivoting and growing, central to this is how and when you do sales to ensure you grow and you attract your ideal market.

About Baiju Solanki
CEO & Founder of EnSpirit Global

Baiju is the CEO and founder of EnSpirit Global: a platform that serves to inspire, educate and connect the entrepreneurial spirit in all of those who wish to live their best life. In addition an award-winning businessman and TEDx speaker.

A trained psychologist, lecturer, speaker and author, he empowers people to achieve their power. Using his skills as a trainer, teacher and coach he aims to transform the world through teaching entrepreneurial skills to business people, students and employees through the EnSpirit platform.

As a former Businessman of The Year, and property investor, his experience extends beyond the realm of enterprise.

Baiju is also an author of #1 Amazon Best Seller *Change Your Game: How to To Achieve Your Potential as an Entrepreneur and Create the Life You Desire* and *I'm An Entrepreneur - Get Me Out of Here*, a selection of interviews with entrepreneurs who talk about the keys to success.

Contact Baiju Solanki

www.EnSpirit.Global

www.ChangeYourGameBook.com

www.ChangeYourGameAccelerator.com

Social Media Links

https://twitter.com/BaijuSolanki

https://www.facebook.com/baiju.solanki

https://www.linkedin.com/in/baijusolanki/

https://www.instagram.com/baijusolanki/

https://www.youtube.com/user/baijusolanki/videos

TEDx Talk

https://www.youtube.com/watch?v=HA-TFRXRWPY&t=48s

It Might Be Lonely At The Top It Certainly Isn't Quiet

Kim-Adele Platts

Our world was already changing; we knew this.

Business is beset by change on all sides. Technology. Competition. Regulations. Politics. The rise of Millenials and their expectations will influence the companies they build, which was before, the impacts of the global pandemic.

Now as well as leading our people through the myriad of challenges, furlough, redundancy, remote working and return to the office, there is the additional challenge of how we pivot and grow our business.

We have always known it is lonely at the top, but it certainly isn't quiet. With so much noise, it is hard to find a focus on what is essential.

As we have seen the world over, we are in the midst of a global leadership crisis, which is providing us with opportunities to learn and develop. As leaders, we understand our responsibility to provide the right care support and guidance for our people. What we are learning is to do this; we also need to get the proper support and guidance for ourselves.

In a recent article on research for LinkedIn, Benjamin Laker (2020) highlighted 69% of C-Suite Leaders had found it the most challenging time to lead with 52% doubting their ability and 41% experiencing higher levels of stress and anxiety. It is not surprising that leaders are finding it a challenge, leading themselves and their people through challenge and uncertainty effectively. See Laker (2020) *Linkedin-research-reveals-rise-of-executive-imposter-syndrome.Forbes*

As we move into the new world and the constant change, the always-on society the need to engage, empower and enthuse our people becomes critical, and our ability to do this rests on our emotional intelligence and ability to connect with people.

As leaders, business owners, we are faced with the responsibility to keep the business going, and that can lead to us becoming too heavily focused on the task rather than the person. We can be looking in the wrong direction; we focus on what we need rather than put ourselves in the shoes of our people and our customers. To understand how to pivot, ask yourself what is it my customer wants and needs? Then think about what your people will need to make that change.

We can become conscious that we are in people's homes and uncomfortable that we might not usually be invited there and so the conversation becomes about the task rather than the person and what they need.

The old *What do I need from my people* style of leadership

being is long gone, and we now need to focus on *What do my people need from me to thrive?*

We have had decades of leading based on the more traditional route of management. We tell people what to do rather than inspire them. Moving forward into the evolving world of digitalisation and artificial intelligence, our ability to use our emotional intelligence rather than just our intellect will be the deciding factor in our ability to remain relevant and obtain real success.

Emotional intelligence is going to be a critical skill, as we have new generations of millennials who are looking for influential leaders who inspire them to work rather than command them to.

So what benefits are there for you and or your organisation to lead with more 'humanity'?

1. You will become more connected to your people and foster an inclusive culture which propels your business forward.
2. You will no longer need to worry about attracting and retaining key talent as your workers would remain committed to your combined cause.
3. You will see significant improvements on your bottom line through reduced attrition, absence and hiring costs alone.
4. You will have a combined sense of belonging and a drive for a common purpose.
5. You will have more robust, more mutually beneficial relationships with your employees, your customers and your partners and suppliers.

The benefits speak for themselves, so what skills do you need to thrive?

Be Present

Have you ever wondered how 'truly present' we are in our day-to-day role as a leader? We have the opportunity in every situation to walk our talk. As leaders, we can look for those opportunities where we are disconnected, the early warning signs that something is not quite right. It helps to understand that while our reputation gets us into the room, it's our character that will keep it there.

Really Listen

While we have already achieved levels of success and leadership, we need to to remain present, particularly when it comes to listening. Too often, we listen to interject rather than to understand, which means we miss the opportunity to learn. If we instead listen to understand the other person, their wants, needs and dreams, then we become better placed to serve them.

Own Your Legacy

We are all leaving an imprint on the world; we all have the potential to leave a lasting legacy. We leave an impression on the world with every conversation and every interaction, but is it the imprint we wish to leave? Leadership can be challenging at the best of times and very often, the concept of 'legacy' lies in the bucket of 'nice to have', but not a necessity, since a company faces so many other priorities.

We all are aware of the popularisation of Simon Sinek's Ted Talk 'How Great Leaders Inspire' and the critical importance of your WHY! Legacy is part of your WHY! To not know your legacy impacts not only yourself but your business!

Build Your Culture

As leaders, the legacy we leave is an integral part of our culture. It is about how we attract and retain talent. People join organisations based on their values, purpose and aspirations. Nevertheless, we know that a significant factor in their decision to join and an even bigger part of the reason they leave is because of their boss.

We know that people don't leave a company; they leave their boss.

Ask yourself, what are you doing every day to make sure your talent is compelled to stay with you?

Gain Clarity

As the quote says, *If you don't know where you're going, any path will take you there*. Our subconscious brain deals with millions and millions of things daily; our conscious mind can only handle between 7 and 9.

If you aren't clear about your direction if you can't see it, hear it and smell it, then your subconscious brain may very well filter out opportunities and never bring them to your conscious mind because it doesn't know that it's important to you. You have to have real clarity, understand precisely where it is you want to go, and only then will your subconscious brain go and find you the opportunities/evidence you need and bring those into your line of sight.

Take Control Of Your Thinking

Our subconscious brain is the most productive helper we will ever have. However, it doesn't understand the difference between positive and negative. Consequently, it assumes whatever we are thinking about, is what we desire or require, and it searches for opportunities to give us more of the same. If we look for positives, we will end up discovering positives, and likewise, if we look for negatives, we would find negatives. We simply become what we think about, so I recommend that we set our goals and our thoughts in the positive – Understand what is it we want, and Focus on it!

Inspire And Create A Compelling Story

People look up to their leader to inspire them to achieve more and develop a culture of inclusivity, creativity and fulfilment.The common trait in those that inspired was their belief in those they lead, their ability to recognise a skill, a strength or a natural talent and to allow it to shine, to nurture, grow and evolve.

The most inspiring leaders I have met have a genuine interest in people and in learning more about them. They have the confidence to understand they are not great at everything and the strength of character to recruit a team around them skilled in the areas they are not.

Build Your Support Network

Leader's have a big job to fill, achieving all this and navigating the challenges and opportunities facing the organisation. I recommend that all leaders also audit their support network. Do you have the support you need to succeed? Remember that you can't pour from an empty cup, your business and your people need you, which means that leading with kindness, humanity and courage starts in the mirror, you have to look after you too.

Having worked at the C-suite level for more than two decades specialising in cultural/organisational transformation for major organisations globally, I have seen that those conscious companies that respected the 'human quotient' time and time again achieved superior results. For me the leadership message is a clear one, what do my people need from me to thrive, by giving them that they will deliver what your customers need which will deliver your business growth.

About Kim-Adele Platts

Kim-Adele Platts FInstLM is an Interim CEO, entrepreneur and board-level coach who specialises in helping executives lead with impact and humanity. Her journey has taken her from an NVQ in hairdressing to the boardrooms of the FTSE 250, navigating plot twists along the way which embedded the importance of the core values of 'humanity, kindness and courage' for her.

Bringing these values into the leadership arena or to the boardroom table has sparked her champion human potential to new levels. She is also a mother to a beautiful daughter who drives her daily to live life to the fullest and leave a legacy that matters.

A world-renowned leadership coach, an internationally bestselling author, inspirational keynote speaker, and master coach, she couples 25 years in the corporate world, with lessons she has garnered throughout her amazing and unique life story, to help others achieve sustainable transformation for professional and personal success.

Contact Kim-Adel Platts

https://kimadele.org

https://www.linkedin.com/in/kimadele/

https://twitter.com/kimadele10

https://www.instagram.com/kimadele10

https://www.facebook.com/kimadele.org

There's Opportunity In Each Hardship We Face

Ben Taylor

If you take only one message from my chapter, it should be the following: there's opportunity in each and every hardship we face. The full scope of this statement is clear, only if we understand that opportunity resides in unresolved challenges, can we attempt to respond, adapt and exploit this opportunity. These hardships are the pain-points that kick-start action.

If this is your only take away from this chapter, I'm happy this will provide more value to you than I could ever hope to communicate to someone so quickly.

To give you some perspective, I'm a young entrepreneurial marketeer, who is tech savvy and a sucker for a good opportunity. I market technologies to the marine industry internationally. This sector is dominated by old strategies, traditional mindsets and undeniably difficult clientele that we call High Net Worth Individuals (HNWIs).

Within marine leisure and yachting sectors, the overarching

marketing strategy revolves around boat shows. Whilst they present a huge cost, they form the driving force behind industry consumption. Venues sell boats, yachts and all the complementary goods that go along with them. It turns out boat shopping is fun, so we make an event out of it!

The trouble is, they aren't taking place, *due to the pandemic*. This, the famous phrase, which is rapidly becoming my most hated, is however, where it gets exciting. Yes, I meant exciting. It is exciting, intriguing and genuinely interesting! The cancellation of boat shows presents huge challenges and hence an array of opportunities.

I've observed two distinct approaches to marketing since boat shows have stopped taking place and consumer behaviour has been forced to shift. One being motivated by concern for ongoing costs, the other being driven by market potential and market share. At this point in time, I firmly support the long-term market potential vision. I hate to be miserable but this is going to take a while to blow over and I have a terrible feeling this isn't going to be the last global pandemic we see. Both approaches, however, have solid reasoning. There were simply too many unknowns within the business landscape we faced at the start of the pandemic, resulting in a split between the adoption of long-term and short-term strategies.

The short-term, cost-conscious strategy favours delay. Temporary cost saving measures are made which increase efficiency and provide a financial buffer before coming into serious difficulties. Thus, this system sacrifices market potentials until marketing systems receive the investment required to attain results. This approach fails in the long term, after all, you're gutting your business of an essential function.

It's unreasonable to expect the same level of success.

Here's the long-term approach in one sentence. Shift your marketing systems to match the shift in consumer behaviour. This allows you to continue developing business and to increase market share. Consumer behaviour may appear unpredictable but don't get too hooked on details, address the underlying behavioural patterns, then refine the strategy to address the superficial behaviour.

An overarching movement is taking place towards digital communication channels, especially in marketing. How's that for a golden nugget? This was already taking place, it's simply been accelerated during the pandemic, I'd say it's accelerated the marine industry's use of digital communications both internally and externally at least five years ahead of where it was, perhaps ten. Even simple automation provides exponential value as time progresses.

Digital marketing systems are high value propositions for obvious reasons, but they're also reliable. Reliability and predictability are both factors that present risk to face-to-face marketing ventures. You should re-evaluate the prospect of investing in newly high-risk ventures like in-person events, trade shows and anything that could be completely undermined through no fault of organisers or of course your own: *due to the pandemic*.

Never underestimate how late, or how devastating the restriction *due to the pandemic* can be. Our industry saw the cancellation of a boat show on the eve of the launch. The reality hit home as a contact of mine saw a parade of boats fleeing the show once the news was made public. This was so last-minute in fact, that many attendees of the show arrived, still anticipating a launch. Not knowing there was no show taking place. There is no doubt that exhibiting multiple yachts, some of which may be 50 feet or more, is a considerable investment risk. It's fair to say the organisers had a lot to answer for. As individual businesses these events are undeniably high-risk budget allocations.

This is where I see opportunities emerging. Opportunities which may be moulded to your business through solid strategy to engage your prospects: podcasts, radio station exposure, webinars, social media and online events - especially networking events, all hold potential. There are many more existing and emerging channels, each of which have their own merits. I would encourage any business to explore them, be informed, and position themselves on the right side of the knowledge gap. Ultimately, only you can determine what level of value these could provide to your business. These are all highly accessible media to any business or an individual. Each holds the capability to engage your audience no matter what pandemic related restrictions are in place.

Oh, and apparently co-authoring a book helps too.

These channels collectively form touchpoints that your prospects can continue to engage with, therefore maintaining or even developing brand equity, it's difficult to measure but with consistency the results will come. Brand equity will determine the recovery rate of businesses post-pandemic. Align your messaging with customer values and they will come flooding back as soon as they can.

Slow moving, big business with long sale cycles is starting to be impacted as pipeline sales are drying up. As many of these projects are driven by personal relationships, we must open our minds to new approaches, including adapting our marketing strategies to align with the new normal.

By this point, technological progressions are being accelerated to address each hurdle an organization faces. Notably, virtual reality technology is undergoing mass adoption as its uses are exploding in value, and in scale. We owe it to ourselves to utilize the opportunity that technology presents.

- Why not have a virtual showroom? Do you know how to build one?
- Do you know how expensive, or should I say inexpensive, it can be?
- Why limit your business to a local or national market? Operate internationally.

What I like to call a 'next generation approach' must be taken whether we like it or not. A next generation approach simply lacks the limitations a traditional approach is restricted to. Think opportunity and future potential rather than what has been, and is no longer. It's a brutal reality that we must come to terms with.

Even as a biased superfan of technology and digital marketing, I recognise the importance of, and still support a hybrid approach for a winning marketing strategy. More so than ever, an omni-channel strategy which incorporates face-to-face interactions, alongside digital channels, offers immense value with a balance of risk and potential gain. With this your business becomes largely independent to pandemic related factors, it forms a robust and powerful asset that will continue to accumulate value over time. This also aligns with emerging sectors which are set to become powerhouses of commerce, namely artificial intelligence, data processing and virtual reality.

It's easy to make this sound, well, easy. Make no mistake these transformations demand an organization to be resourceful. It's somewhat comforting that we all face the same foe, I feel there's a camaraderie around this which we can all leverage for collaborations; the value of which has only been enhanced by the disruption. I find companies being more open to cooperation as people move away from rigid thinking towards open minded entrepreneurial synergies. So, share resources, identify assets that could complement each other and expand the value you both extract from them. Be sure to extend this openness to other industries as they may offer a whole wealth of insight that's simply not communicated to your sector particularly well.

Through resourcefulness, the future points to great possibilities. Whilst we're experiencing immense change many jump to pessimistic conclusions. We must challenge ourselves to adapt to the landscape that lies ahead.

Close the knowledge gap, invest in new ventures, have faith in brand equity, explore emerging technologies, accommodate for behavioural change and truly embrace the opportunity we all have.

Remember, there's opportunity in each hardship we face. Evaluate, strategize and execute.

About Ben Taylor

Ben Taylor is a young entrepreneurial marketeer who specialises in marketing technology to the marine leisure and superyacht industries globally. He runs his own marketing company Taylor Digital Ltd, based near Manchester, UK. He's part of the British Marine federation and hosts his own radio show "Flagship Digital Insights" on Yachting International Radio. When Ben isn't attending boat shows you may find him on the water wakeboarding or under the water freediving. On rare occasions away from water he'll be exploring new business ventures, public speaking, playing the piano or skiing in the Alps. Ben is an advocate for networking and prides himself on connecting with people through his international network of industry experts, collaborators and close friends.

Contact Ben Taylor

Website: *www.ben-taylor.digital*

LinkedIn: *www.linkedin.com/in/ben-taylor-digital-marine*

How Web Pivoted And Grew

Alexander Seery

The six most expensive words in business are, *We've always done it that way* and the total cost is your growth and the success of your business.

Innovation and change are essential when it comes to achieving your vision for your business. Now more than ever, due to the 2020 global pandemic, it is critical.

If you never innovate or change the way you do things, you will never improve and with this comes a road to mediocrity and empty bank balances.

I am the founder and CEO of a business training company that supports members of the public sector in starting and scaling successful business, as well as the best-selling author of a business book called Police Officer to Entrepreneur.

When the 2020 global pandemic came about, but more specially during the lockdown period enforced in an effort to flatten the curve, I gathered my team for an urgent meeting. This meeting was not just about surviving, it was about growing beyond measure, not only through the global pandemic but also through the inevitable recession.

We run live in-person events which were disrupted due to the lockdown. This put pressure on us being able to serve our clients whilst also disrupting our sales process.

There were some key discussion within this meeting, however for the purpose of this book, I will point out the areas where I think will add the most value as well how we PIVOTED and GREW.

1. Contingency Planning

When an astronaut goes into space, they are not jumping for joy, thanking the heavens they get to see the moon and the stars from the international space station. They are checking for faults and flaws with their equipment and space craft. They are checking to see if they have enough oxygen, food, and water at all stages of their journey. They are checking their space suit as well as their tech. They are contingency planning.

In the meeting with my team, we thought of the worst-case scenario. *What if we were locked down for two or more years? What would happen if we could never run events again? What if we did not make another sale during this pandemic? What if we can't support our clients?.*

With these questions, it allowed us to contingency plan on fixing these types of problems by reframing them into *How* type questions, for example, *How can we run events? How can we make sales during this pandemic? How can we still support our customers?*

By reframing them into *How* type questions it allowed our creative mindsets to utilise its problem-solving abilities.

By simply asking *how*, your brain goes into problem solving mode. This allowed us to start thinking of creative solutions.

2. Decision Making

From our team meeting, there were some amazing ideas that came about which I am grateful for. However, I had to make some big decisions and I knew that ultimately these decisions would alter the future of my company. I believe decisiveness yields its own rewards. You must act prudently and with haste. It is better to find yourself wrong quickly than never to move at all because indecision can cost you more than the wrong decision.

But one key factor that helped me in the decision-making process was my company's vision:

"To be the world's most prestigious business training company that creates transformational life experiences for the public sector through entrepreneurial ideas".

Were the changes I was about to make for my company in alignment with its vision? The ideas that were not were put on the shelf, and the ideas what were, we acted upon.

3. Customer Feedback

It's all well and good coming up with ideas to fix problems that occur in business, but when you're coming up with a completely new innovation of your product it's important to know what your customers think before you implement.

The changes we made for our core product, which is a business accelerator, was first put together on paper and based on previous feedback from customers who had been through the old version. With the new concept we always kept in mind supporting our customers and providing value in a remarkable way. I was not willing to sacrifice this within the changing process.

Adapting from the feedback and not deterring from our vision in supporting our customers in building successful business, I put together a slide deck showcasing the new changes we were making to our core product, which was named Shifts to Success 2.0.

It highlighted the features and benefits of Shifts to Success 2.0, but more importantly the outcomes it could provide, which is why our customers were really buying from us.

I then screen recorded the slide deck which I conducted a presentation, talking over all the various points, features, and benefits, and published this video within our community, asking for customer feedback on the new product concept.

Once I did this, I was carefully reading all the comments, which thankfully they were positive, supportive, and constructive, giving me more ideas to make the concept better. I also took the time to speak to existing clients over the phone and zoom and gathered their thoughts and impressions of the revised core product. This allowed me to take a more calculated risk for the new product launch – Shifts to Success 2.0.

4. Promotion & Signalling Interest

Our next step was to create and distribute digital assets to our market that allowed us to promote our new product launch. We created infographics, a new product image, more client case studies/testimonials, and an inspiring video in which I explained exactly what our business accelerator is and who it is for.

Myself and my team also selected a date in which we would take our first intake of new customers on board the new Shifts to Success 2.0 Accelerator.

We also created a priority list in which our potential customers could join if they were interested in enrolling. By doing this it allowed us to gauge their level of interest, but also reassured us that there is interest from new customers who we have not yet had the pleasure to support.

By gathering a priority list of potential customers, it also allowed us to create supply demand tension, meaning that not everyone who joined would be able to join our new Accelerator, which created buying urgency and it separated the warm leads from the hot leads. This is helpful is it allowed me to know where to focus my time.

5. Sales

After gathering interest on the priority list, I then took the time to speak to each prospect and carefully listen to their problems, challenges, and frustrations. I allowed them to speak 70-80% of the time and I directionally adjusted the conversation with my questions.

By taking the time to understand the prospects I was

speaking to, I was also able qualify them in or out. I wanted to make sure that we have the right people on our Accelerator as maintaining a great culture is of top priority within Shifts to Success.

We sold out our first intake, bringing in £36,000 in sales for the first launch. Although sales are the life blood of every business, I think it is important to note that the aim here was to first ensure we were supporting customers, solving their problems, and giving them what they wanted. It is not about taking someone's money; it is about starting a relationship and helping your customer to a better future.

Where are we now?

We have now successful pivoted and grown during the global pandemic and things have changed for the better.

We have done this in several ways.

1. Online Portal

When customers enrol in our Accelerator, they gain access to our online learning portal. The online portal allows them to move through each of the business lessons and modules so they can start or scale their business. Everything our team teaches them is in the online Masterclasses which they can access within the portal. Also included are downloadable resources such as business plans, financial spreadsheets, cheat sheets and a variety of other templates which support each stage of the Accelerator. In addition, they can also watch all our previous webinars and bonus teachings on-demand, and they gain access to our trusted suppliers.

2. Online Mentor Masterclasses

During the Accelerator our customer will thrive by having access to regular online Masterclass Workshops hosted by the Shifts to Success Approved Mentors. Our team is made up of exceptional individuals who are experts in the Shifts to Success business builder model. During these interactive, in-depth, online Masterclasses, we walk our customers through each step of building their business with practical advice to take away and implement in their own businesses. This is done in a safe and supportive environment with their fellow Cohort members.

3. Cohort Facebook Community

This community is for our customers only. When they start their Accelerator, they will join former members and the Shifts to Success Mentors in our supportive private Facebook community. Within this community, they can share all their wins, gain feedback, share their challenges, ask for advice and network with those who are on the same journey as them.

4. Accountability Coaches

During their Accelerator, our members will be assigned to their very own Accountability Coach. These are highly driven accountability groups led by a Shifts to Success Top Performer. (A top performer is a customer who has achieved amazing results personally and professionally through our accelerator) These environments ensure they are being held to account in completing their business tasks, which take them towards their goals quicker than they ever imagined possible.

This benefits our customers in a number of ways such as:

- They no longer need to travel to gain insights on how to start and scale a business.
- They save on travel costs and expenses such as hotels.
- The online masterclasses are shorter in length which helps to avoid overwhelm and retain information better.
- The regular online masterclasses with our mentors allows them to take the class again and again until they have mastered their specific area of building a business.
- Regular accountably means they get to move forwards towards their goals consistently.
- The online portal has assessments built in which means our members cannot progress forwards without first mastering one area of building a business. This gives structure and direction.
- We have now gone from a 12-month accelerator to now and on-going support accelerator no matter where our clients are in their journeys.

Since we have pivoted, the results have been astonishing, and we are only just getting started! The changes have allowed us to make a bigger impact and give additional support to our customers, which are all in alignment with our vision. Not only that, but these changes have allowed us to go global and we now work with international clients.

Before the global pandemic, we were making an impact

with 50 customers per year by enrolling them onto our Accelerator. Within a 7-month period since lockdown, we have gained 59 customers already and are projected to have 125 customers within 12 months. This projection would yield a 150% increase.

I believe everything in life can push or prevent you, however, you are the one who always determines the outcome. There is opportunity to be had during this global pandemic and recession as well as many lessons along the way.

The question is, will you allow this to push you or prevent you? Will you pivot and grow?

About Alexander Seery

Alexander Seery is a best selling author and successful entrepreneur. At the age of 24, he built his first company with zero start-up capital to a six-figure business while working full time as an officer based in custody.

Alex is also founder and CEO of Shifts to Success, a specialised business training company that supports public sector workers to start and scale successful businesses. Learn more at *www.shiftstosuccess.com*

Pivot And Grow To Stay Relevant

Dave Clare

Pivot and Grow is a deceptive title for this little ripper of a book. It sounds like a survival guide for reactionary leaders that realise they need to change their business direction if they want to grow the business to survive. Then you read the subtitle and see the words "creating a sustainable steady growth business" and release a sigh of relief. It is about a process or a relationship with pivoting for growth and not a reactionary transaction.

This chapter is about having a proactive approach to pivoting and growing. It is about evolving your business to stay relevant in the hearts and minds of the people you choose to serve. Pivoting and growing are core to the process of evolution. Evolution, by its own nature, is a continuing process of change from one state or condition to another or from one form to another.

You pivot and grow. You pivot again and grow some more. You pivot again and grow even more. By design. You continue to evolve and stay relevant.

Simple.

Let's start with my love hate relationship with the word pivot. I hate it when leaders, owners and entrepreneurs say they need to pivot the business, but I love it when a business pivots on purpose.

May I start by suggesting what a pivot or pivoting is not.

It is not pivoting when you digitize your distribution channel of the same product or service to the same people in the same market. If I had a dollar for every "We need to pivot to online" I would not have to be a contributing author to this book. I would be pivoting my lifestyle to living on a beach somewhere in the Bahamas with all those dollars.

Leaders may choose to pivot their business for a multiple of reasons. I believe there are a couple of key reasons to choose to pivot. As a Canadian, hockey is in our blood, so I will insert this well used hockey quote here, and then provide context after.

"Skate to where the puck is going, not where it has been."

- Walter Gretzky

This advice has been popularized by former NHL player and legend, Wayne Gretzky, but it is from his father Walter. It is a simple concept, but what is missing is that it requires a tremendous ability to read the play and increase your odds of being where the puck will end up.

The first, and best time, is by design. An intentional pivot to stay ahead of the market, your market, or move to where the market is headed. Look at where your customers' customers are headed. That should help you anticipate and strategize where your clients will head and where you can be of service and remain relevant to them.

I am always interested in this concept. Why?

"If you don't start anticipating the future needs of your customers, the one thing you can anticipate is not having future customers."
- a Clarism

The second reason to pivot on purpose is also by design to move into a new market because you see an opportunity, a gap that allows you to diversify or expand with a new offering and/or to new clients.

One of the most famous pivots in this space was Starbucks. When Howard Schultz, then an employee of Starbucks, went on a business trip to Italy back in 1983, he fell in love with the barista experience, the symphony of community and enjoying coffee together in Italy. In an interview with Oprah Winfrey, Schultz advised that upon coming back to America he realised Starbucks was in the wrong business. He helped pivot Starbucks from a coffee maker and coffee beans sales organisation into the fastest growing café/coffee shop in North America… and the rest is, as they say, history.

The worst reason to pivot is because you are being forced too.

When you react, or pivot for survival it is usually because you weren't paying attention to any of the other two reasons and you now have reached crisis stage and need to do something just to survive.

This begs the question then, how do we build our business so that pivoting to grow is the natural state of our business? How do we ensure that we are able to anticipate, identify and adapt to our ever-changing environment?

Yes, Darwin theories tell us that it is not the fastest, the fittest, the smartest or strongest that survives. It is the one most able to adapt to their EVER-CHANGING environment.

That means you must choose to affect change or be at the mercy of the effects of change.

Why?

"Every business model has a shelf life.
Has yours expired and you just don't know it yet?"
- a Clarism

In a more technical sense, a pivot is a reasonable shift in one or more of your business model attributes. Who? What? How? Where? When?

You may notice that I did not mention Why?

Why you do should not change much, but how and what you do (and who for) can and always will change. You will have a model business that may have several business models over its lifetime of evolution.

To proactively implement pivots appropriately into your business evolution, you will need to challenge your strategic thinking. As owners, leaders, and entrepreneurs in an uncertain world, it is critical to test our strategic thinking. How we have done strategy in the past will not serve us going forward.

Now is the time to challenge how we lead. We should be questioning if our culture and strategy are aligned? Now more than ever, Entrepreneurs seeking to raise capital for their business need to demonstrate they have a Model Business, not just a Business Model.

If you want your business to remain relevant into the future, it needs to evolve.

You cannot keep doing what you are doing and expect to survive, let alone thrive. When you start to think of the strategy for the next evolution of your business, and the possible pivots to make, the best way to discover it is to ask an epic question. Epic questions produce epic thinking and that leads to epic actions and epic results.

"When was the last time you sat down and thought about how to put yourself out of business? I assure you; your competitors are thinking about it right now."
- a Clarism

When you put yourself out of business, you are merely putting your old way of doing business out. When someone else puts you out of business... you are out of business.

Take yourself out of your business. Go across the street and look back at your business and imagine:

"If we set up a new business here, how would we put (Insert your business name here)out of business?"

You have a choice. Again, you can choose to affect change or be at the mercy of the effects of change.

By design or by default? Which do you choose?

The concept of pivot and grow is about your ability to make pivoting part of your natural strategic process to enable your business to evolve to stay relevant in the hearts and minds of the people you choose to serve… now and in the future.

About Dave Clare

Dave works with SME leaders to productively transform their lives and businesses to evolve to stay relevant in the heart and minds of the people they serve. He is the CEO & Founder of Circle Leadership and Ambassador (Pacific Region) for the GLOBAL Company Culture Association dedicated to driving an evolution at work.

Combining practical experience in corporate and NFP leadership roles with running his own SME business internationally, Dave developed a proven online, transparent framework to develop and execute an aligned strategy to enable businesses to become radically client-centric.

He is a trained facilitator with two international organisations, and a qualified mentor with the RCSA Pearl and Inspiring Rare Birds programs for female leaders in Australia.

A sought-after speaker and MC, Dave is the author of SIMPLIFIED, and creator of the Leadership Framework©, the Circle of Organizational Leadership©, the Model Business Canvas©, and the Culture and Strategy Advance©.

Contact Dave Clare

www.daveclare.com

www.globalcompanycultureassociation.com

www.leadershipsipmlified.com

www.linkedin.com/in/prophetforpurpose

Normalise Challenges And Change

Andrew Priestley

Pivot

My very first business was selling salt and pepper shakers door-to-door. Soul destroying. Then I started a Saturday mowing round which finally gave me serious pocket money to buy MAD magazines, bubble gum cards and model airplanes.

At uni I started a folk club because I was playing guitar and was into folk music. At first, it was just pure traditional and contemporary folk music i.e., folk songs, jigs and reels, protest songs etc. But it wasn't viable. I realized I could get more people if I broadened it out to *acoustic* music where you could enjoy any popular music, unplugged.

Quickly, I had larger audiences and needed bigger venues. That business lasted while I was at university.

I went to Deakin University in Australia and actually started the student newspaper, *The Planet* where I learned how to publish. Publishing ink got into my veins.

In the early 1980s, a mate bought back both a health and surfing newspapers from the US. So I decided to start both a holistic lifestyle, *and* a surfing newspaper. And because I loved live music I created a rock press newspaper called *The Mix*. All funded by advertising.

I quickly discovered that the holistic and surfing newspaper - while really good concepts - had a very limited advertising revenue base. But the music newspaper thrived because live entertainment pubs and clubs needed a gig guide. So I dropped the health and surfing titles.

I soon realized there wasn't enough market or money to support *another* dedicated rock music magazine so I pivoted into a lifestyle publication called *Big Night Out* (BNO). My timing was really good. People had more disposable income and were more sophisticated and were hungry for hospitality, fashion, film, the arts and cultural options.

But despite rapid growth, I was working 12-14 hour days, seven days a week. After six months, I realised the irony of running a lifestyle publication where I was stressed, exhausted and close to burn out. I made the decision to shut that business down.

I contemplated on where the most value had been delivered for my clients. It was in creating advertising and ad campaigns that worked. I was actually very good at writing ad copy.

I did a marketing degree, several National Advertising Bureau of Australia (NABA) courses run by Jim Moffat and Jim Alexander who had worked with the greats - John Caples, David Ogilvy and Claude Hopkins!

I pivoted into a family-friendly advertising agency. I focused on copywriting and designing ads which was better paid, more profitable and a better fit for family life.

Then I merged with another agency and started to specialize in strategic marketing. I realised that while I could write ads for clients, I discovered there was no point doing a great ad unless I knew where that ad fitted into their overall marketing strategy.

So, a pivot from advertising into marketing.

That led into business development with a focus on revenues, sustainable growth, and profitability.

I stopped servicing small business clients and I started to focus on established SMEs with more sophisticated needs, bigger budgets and longer more profitable relationships.

And we started winning awards.

And some of my clients would ask, *Can I have a coffee with you?* because they wanted to know how to grow a business. And so I started making more money from advisory services.

And out of that I became a business coach.

Very quickly I was in the top 2% of fee earning business coaches on the planet working with established businesses with revenues north of USD$2m.

I had also gone back to uni and done an industrial and organisation psychology degree and my focus started to shift to working exclusively with the business owner and business leadership coaching.

I went from charging hundreds of dollars, to thousands of dollars then tens of thousands of dollars. And I went from serving a customer base of 3,500 clients down to working with just 30-40 clients a year.

I still do BDM and strategic work but the focus is on

executive leadership coaching and mentoring where instead of skills development I am working with your bigger purpose and intentions; your identity as a business leader; and your beliefs and values.

Notice that my business has pivoted through many iterations but each time I was building on strong skill sets.

Grow

Be clear each iteration had clear growth targets. As the revenues grew, I also had to grow the profits, resources, staff, customers, products and services etc.

So, my career over 35 years plus has been one of pivot, grow, pivot, grow: those two things always working together.

You could say that the pivots were mostly organic in the sense that as I learned things, I naturally developed and evolved my value propositions. So yes, a natural progression.

But I want to say there were many times when I had to pivot and grow, on demand.

I bet you've been through some of the same business challenges and challenging times, too. I bet you've experienced downturns, recessions, inflation; and fast growth, technology changes and trends like globalisation etc. Remember the global financial crisis (GFC)? Brexit? And now a pandemic?

Those events forced me to really understand money management and how money flows through business.

One of my side hustles as a business coach is teaching business owners about how management accounts work, for example.

While its profitable, I will not pivot in that direction because that is more akin to being an accountant.

Each tough time, I've had to go out and find business. I've had to look at my product and service mix and I've had to adjust and adapt these products or services. In some cases that meant either bundling or unbundling services and lowering (or increasing) my prices to win customers.

Under these conditions, it needs to be deliberate and conscious.

In some cases, I had to go right back to my roots - door-to-door selling - relying on those skills of networking, staying in touch and hustling to find and retain clients.

Pivoting and change can be *remedial* (small), *adaptive* (medium) or *proactive* (large wholesale). Like me, I suspect you've made all three, too.

Right now, I'm seeing people who are making remedial changes like bundling or unbundling their products and services. Or they're adapting by taking something previously delivered offline by taking it online. Or by turning complex services into one-off events, sprints or workshops. Or by adopting new technologies. Or by creating modified retainers or packages. Or by redesigning the customer journey.

And I've seen clients pivot into whole new businesses. Understand though, at any level, they were pivoting on an existing proven strengths. People who pivoted into totally unfamiliar unrelated areas, typically stall or fail.

Normalise Change

I've been in business a long time. I want to encourage you to normalize the fact that your business is constantly facing challenges and is constantly changing. It might be going through an organic evolution or it might be forced by necessity as we are witnessing currently. Pay attention to what is needed and what works. It might only be remedial changes that you have to make. But it might be adaptive or proactive changes that are needed.

If you need to change, change.

I had a mate in the US running an event management company, that suddenly can't put 3,000 people in a venue, but nor 300 or even 30! Not changing took that business to the wall, because they were first resistant and then too slow to respond.

By contrast, my son, whose business relied on a venue-based delivery model, successfully pivoted and adapted rapidly to online presentations. As I'm writing, super coach, Tony Robbins, has pivoted from doing 10,000 person super mega live arena events to taking all that online.

Challenges are normal. So expect them. You need to determine whether you need to make remedial, adaptive, or wholesale proactive changes to your business. And notice whether those changes are leading to profitable growth.

I had a friend who was doing £1m in revenues. His overheads were £900k and let's say his net profit was £100k. He pivoted and grew to £1.2m, but costs grew to £1.1m, so net profits were still only £100k!

A pivot has to make sense.

I have a client who is pivoting from a global refrigeration logistics company into a *green* research and development company because solid research grants are there. In his case, revenues will grow gradually, but it will instantly be a lot more profitable - and smarter - for them to become an R&D company.

It's a natural progression and the pivot builds on existing value.

Again, I want to emphasise: normalise challenges. Normalise change. Just reflect carefully on whether it needs to be remedial, adaptive or proactive.

And consider how you will measure the impact of the pivot and the changes. How will you know its working? What will *good* look like if everything *conservatively* goes as planned?

Whether it's organic or demanded it has to be conscious, deliberate and intentional.

Having done strategic business development for a long time now, scenario planning and stress testing assumptions requires scrupulous thought in order to best determine when, where and how you should pivot in order to achieve sensible, sustainable growth. And maybe how to fail faster and pivot again if you fall short of your current best thinking.

I hope that helps.

About Andrew Priestley

Andrew Priestley mentors entrepreneur leaders worldwide. He is qualified in industrial and organisations; psychology, is an award winning business coach, bestselling author and an in demand speaker.

He is the Chairman of *Clear Sky Children's Charity UK* that provides support for vulnerable children aged 4-12 that have witnessed or directly experienced a trauma; and a strategic advisor to *The Mahler Foundation* which promotes the legacy of composer, Gustav Mahler, globally. He is a NXD for several companies.

He loves to cook, draw and play music.

He loves his garden and is a strong advocate of consciously caring for the environment wherever you live.

Contact Andrew Priestley

You can find him on LinkedIn or *www.andrewpriestley.com*

Why not book a 30-Minute Chat:

https://andrewpriestley.as.me

What Does Your Customer *Really* Want?

Afterword: Martin Norbury

The default position of any business is death, a cheery thought, hey.

This means that as business owners, our real role is to keep our businesses alive and the odds are stacked against us. Or are they?

You only have to look at the world and see the businesses that are dominating the financial indexes were not around twenty, ten or even five years ago.

You now have to look quite hard to find successful generational businesses. Recent business history is littered with behemoths businesses that dominated their markets, being suddenly replaced by small, agile disruptors that were not even on their radar.

The classic Netflix v Blockbuster, the demise of Kodak as a market leader, the advent of what I call the asset-leveraged business platform/model.

Uber has no cars, Airbnb has no properties, Facebook doesn't create any content, Deliveroo has no restaurants... currently (watch that space!).

The success of the modern business is not about falling in love with the product or service, it's all about falling in love with the customer and listening to them.

The three words every business owner needs to remember are: Product Market Fit.

I will demonstrate how this expression is the key to sustain, grow and pivot your business into the future.

We are in 2020 and the world is having to cope with a forced change due to the global pandemic. So, let's use this situation as an example of how *Product Market Fit* works.

I have a product that has no brand, no marketing, no website but it works. I have a meeting today with a world leader. My product is the cure for Covid (this is of course made up). How much selling would I have to do? I could set my price for this, and any government would pay for it. *Product Market Fit.*

Five years down the line and there is no Covid, I wouldn't be able to give it away.

This is what pivoting is all about; understanding the demand in the market and solving the problem better than other people do or serving the need better than anybody else does.

The reason Airbnb, Uber, Facebook, Netflix exist is because they looked at the need of the market and provided a better solution than everybody else.

Netflix did the same but did not rest on its position because now it actually makes films and TV series just for Netflix and I'm sure will evolve again.

Pivot and grow are the new mantra for businesses, and the late great Clayton Christensen describes it brilliantly:

> *'The customer has a job to do, and they will hire the best product or service to get it DONE.'*

Facebook, Airbnb, Uber, Netflix etc didn't just succeed because of technology or by replacing an existing product with the same. They got obsessed with the job that the customer wanted doing and developed products and services that did it better than anybody else.

BUT... they didn't fall in love with their product and service, they fell in love with their customer and so continue to pivot and grow by continually asking *what the job is the customer REALLY needs doing.*

For any business owner wanting to succeed on whatever stage they operate on, the best way to reduce the odds of that default position of death is through pivot and growth.

I wish you all the very best.

Martin Norbury

Advocate Business Services

Investor, Mentor, Entrepreneur, Author *I Don't Work Fridays*

https://www.linkedin.com/in/martinjnorbury/

Would You Like To Contribute To Future Editions of *Pivot And Grow?*

If you would like to get involved in the next release of *Pivot and Grow*, then please get in touch. There is a high demand for strategic thinking, globally and readers want your clearest advice, keen insights and sharp mentoring.

If you would like the *Pivot & Grow Writer's Guide*, please email:

coachbiz@hotmail.com

Lightning Source UK Ltd.
Milton Keynes UK
UKHW010637191120
373689UK00002B/500

9 781912 774739